VOICES FROM THE PAST

VOICES FROM THE PAST

History of the English Conference of the
Presbyterian Church of Wales, 1889—1938

by
R. BUICK KNOX, Ph.D.
*Formerly Professor of Ecclesiastical History
in the Theological College, Aberystwyth*

First Impression - January 1969

Printed in Wales by
J. D. Lewis and Sons Ltd., Gomerian Press, Llandyssul

CONTENTS

		Page
I.	Welsh Presbyterianism and its English-speaking Churches	11
II.	Worship and Preaching	27
III.	The Faith of the Church	40
IV.	Church Relations	71
V.	Evangelism and Social Duty	89
VI.	The Church and Politics	108
VII.	The Church and its Young People	122

Appendix : List of Conferences and Conference Personalities .. 135
    „   : Bibliography 137
    „   : Notes 138
Index of Conference Speakers 141

ABBREVIATIONS

References in the text are to the Conference Reports, year and page.

References to English churches indicate the English-speaking churches within Welsh Presbyterianism.

BC : *Y Bywgraffiadur Cymreig hyd* 1940.

CCH : *Cylchgrawn Cymdeithas Hanes (Journal of the Historical Society of the Presbyterian Church of Wales).*

PREFACE

by the Rev. David Williams, B.A.,
Ex-Moderator of the Association in the East

THIS is the Reverend Dr. R. Buick Knox's book.

It was a self-imposed task, and is a very painstaking piece of research, a valuable study of the changes that were taking place at the turn of the century, and of the thought and activities of our Church during an interesting period in its history.

The work was considered to be of such interest that it was decided to publish it to mark the 21st Anniversary of the formation of the Association in the East.

We owe a great debt of gratitude to the author for his labour of assembling, classifying, and catalogueing a great deal of material.

My main duty as editor has been to read the MSS. and with the help and support of the appointed committee, to deal with the publication of this work.

Arrangements for the publication of the book were far advanced when we heard of the resignation of Dr. Knox from the chair of Church History at the Theological College, Aberystwyth, upon his appointment to the Chair in the same subject at Westminster College, Cambridge. We wish him every blessing and happiness in his new sphere.

A word of appreciation is due also to the Gomerian Press, Llandyssul, for an understanding and patient helpfulness beyond a publisher's normal call of duty.

Chapter I

WELSH PRESBYTERIANISM AND ITS ENGLISH-SPEAKING CHURCHES

DURING the past century Wales has undergone great changes in social habit, in economic distribution, and in religious observance, but forecasts about the direction and extent of the changes have often been wide of the mark. Ecclesiastical spokesmen are particularly liable to error both in their woeful prognostications and in their exuberant expectations. Accustomed as they are to dealing with such concepts as the absolute and the eternal they tend to equate their partial judgements with the verdicts of total objectivity. More often than not, they regard current trends as decadent and they make sweeping generalisations on the basis of isolated segments of evidence. Reports of ecclesiastical conferences often make sorry but salutary reading in the light of later events. Nevertheless, such conferences have been valuable sources of inspiration for the faithful, and conference reports contain abundant grain amid the chaff as well as much which, often unwittingly, illustrates the life and thought of the period.

The reports of the many assemblies, Associations and conferences held in connection with Welsh Presbyterianism provide much information about the religious, social and political life of Wales. Welsh Presbyterianism sprang from the movement inaugurated by Howel Harris in 1735.[1] It developed into the Calvinistic Methodist Connexion which is still one of the official names of the denomination. Harris' spiritual descendants have played a significant part in the history of Wales. One of their most formative leaders was Lewis Edwards, educationalist, theologian and administrator.[2]

Edwards was born in 1809 and he grew up within the Connexion when it was predominantly Welsh in language and outlook. He devoted his great gifts to the service of his Church and he largely remodelled it. He brought it into touch with Presbyterianism in other lands and infused a measure of Presbyterianism into its structure. This led to the adoption of the title of the Presbyterian Church of Wales. He also encouraged the policy of settling ministers in pastorates and he was keenly aware of the opportunity for expansion among the growing English-speaking population in the coastal resorts and in areas open to Anglicisation such as Montgomery and Glamorgan. The churches which were founded as a result of this impetus were linked to the Welsh-speaking Associations in North and South Wales. However, these English-speaking churches soon began to feel the need for fellowship among themselves since ministers and elders who could not speak Welsh had to be silent and uncomprehending in the meetings of the Associations.

Tentative moves were made to draw the English churches together in conferences which began in the North at Bangor in 1883 and in the South at Swansea in 1884. They had no legislative power nor did they desire any, at least at the beginning. Many of the leading ministers of English churches were bilingual and they could find an outlet for their administrative gifts in the existing Associations. A further step was taken in 1889 when a conference representative of both North and South was held in Aberystwyth. This was followed by a further united conference in 1892 and thenceforward it became an annual feature until 1938, with the exception of the Great War years, 1914-18.[3]

There were some apprehensions at first lest these Conferences should reduce the prestige of the Associations but the weekly denominational paper, *Y Goleuad*, gave steady encouragement to the venture. It even rebuked some of the denominational leaders for failing to attend the Conferences and deplored the reluctance of some English churches to offer hospitality for the Conference.[4] It could even point out the feebleness of some speeches, especially at the social functions connected with the Conferences.[5] Nevertheless, it did not grudge its praise. After the second Conference in 1892 *Y Goleuad* said that no previous Connexional conference had ever faced up to contemporary problems with greater clarity or honesty.[6] In 1893 the same paper saluted the Conference as "one of the main meetings of the Connexion".[7] In 1894 four pages of *Y Goleuad* were devoted to a report of the Conference. By 1901 the Conference was adjudged to have been the most successful Conference so far held.[8]

A Conference report was published each year, and since the Conference was not a legislative body little of the Reports is taken up with the normal and often dreary details of ecclesiastical administration, but many pages are rich in references to contemporary affairs both inside and outside the confines of the Presbyterian Church of Wales.

The early conferences were generally pervaded by a note of optimism. The number of English churches was increasing rapidly as was also their membership and financial resources and they were regarded as a bridge of contact with the Churches in England (1897, 28). However, it is significant that in 1901 the Rev. Richard Morris, M.A., B.D., Dolgellau, could speak of "the dread century which has just begun" (1901, 30).

It was assumed that the English language was irreversibly in the ascendant and that Welsh was faced with an inevitable decline. There was a somewhat premature assurance that the obituary of the Welsh language would soon be written. In 1893 Rev. J. Calvin Thomas, Hoylake, said, "When Welsh Methodism becomes weak, in the evening of her noble life, when her work is nearly finished, she shall be tenderly nursed and generously supported by her English children" (1839, 9). If there was a somewhat patronising tone in such references there was also the clear-sighted recognition that the spread of the Christian Gospel was of greater importance than the survival of the language. In 1896 Mr. Owen Owen, Headmaster of Oswestry High School, noted that although the number of Welsh speakers had doubled since 1800 yet only one in four of the population of Wales was Welsh-speaking, but he also was not over-anxious, since nationality and language were not inseperable (1896, 14).

In 1897 Rev. R. J. Williams told the Swansea Conference that Wales would become more and more Anglicised (1897, 10). Rev. James Owen, a Baptist, told the same Conference that the loss of the Welsh language was possible but not inevitable (1897, 21). The retiring President of this Conference, Rev. William Evans, Pembroke Dock, spoke of the language of the Church as an accident, but its central task of spreading the Gospel was an abiding aspect of its life. In 1899 Prof. Edwin Williams, M.A., Trevecka, referred to the increasing use of English in Wales and said that the tide could not be stemmed but he had no sympathy for those who despised the Welsh language ; however, he felt equally remote from the "perfervid extravagance which saw the Theology, Hymnology and Hwyl of the Connexion inextricably linked to the Welsh language". In his view the Connexion was founded to save souls and not to preserve the language, and it had a duty to all the inhabitants of Wales, whatever their language (1899, 22). In 1903 Principal Owen Prys said he regretted that the Welsh language was in decline and he blamed parents for not teaching it to their children but he did not think that religion and language were bound together (1903, 9).

However, the transition to English was not as smooth as these references might suggest. In giving a report of the work of the Home Mission in 1899 Rev. J. Glyn Davies said that the work of the Mission was being restricted by the stubborn Welsh adherence to their language; "pitiable attempts are made to stem the English tide and confusion follows"; indeed, an Atlantic passage in winter was not so stormy as the Calvinistic Methodist transition from Welsh to English (1899, 72). In 1906 the President, Rev. Joseph Evans, Denbigh, referred in his valedictory address to "the persistent obstinacy of those in authority to make any change in the language of the ministry", and as a result the young were being lost; many of them had been brought up to speak only English and so could not understand the Welsh services which they attended with their parents. He said he could not blame such young people for leaving the Connexion and said that the language's preservation must not be gained at the cost of the "spiritual welfare of our own flesh and blood" (1906, 20-1). Rev. J. Glyn Davies referred to the same problem in 1909; in many families, only one parent spoke Welsh and the language of the hearth was English but out of traditional family loyalty the family attended Welsh services and children even learned to recite Welsh verses which they did not comprehend. This, in his view, was an unprofitable exercise which neither built up the Church nor preserved the language (1909, 26-7).

Instead of declining, there were speakers after the Great War who discerned an increasing interest in the language, and it has recently been suggested that the ethos and outlook of non-conformity were so closely connected with the Welsh language that an Anglicised version of non-conformity had not sufficient innate vitality to take the place of the native variety.[9] In 1923 Mr. John Owens, J.P., a shrewd observer of the life of the nation spoke of a current revival in "the teaching and maintenance of the Welsh language", and he thought that a place should be given to Welsh in training candidates for the ministry. He noted that this was happening in the Church in Wales which had been "kindled into spiritual energy by its freedom in which we all rejoice" (1923, 8). He nevertheless admitted the difficulties caused to the English churches by the predominance of Welsh in the Connexional courts (1923, 9).

The retiring President, Rev. R. R. Williams, spoke in 1935 about the increasing interest in the language. A government report, *Welsh in Education and Life*, had been published in 1927 and had pointed out the increase of English-speaking residents in North Wales and in the industrial South. Schools had then to cater for more and more monoglots and Welsh was being less used by the young who were consequently unable to follow church services in Welsh, and an ancestral devotion to Welsh would not necessarily survive in the next generation. Churches in Monmouth and Glamorgan had already felt there was little point in continuing to hold services in Welsh and many had changed to English. This was inevitable and there was no justification for continuing to preach in Welsh to the old and middle-aged in the presence of the uncomprehending young. However, in Williams' view, the publication of such a stark report had produced a revived interest in Welsh and had convinced many of the need to take steps to teach it more thoroughly to the young (1935, 15-17).

The tension between English and Welsh usage in the Church was softened by the fact that many ministers of leading English-speaking churches were Welsh-speaking and took a full part in the Conference. The Conference also invited well-known figures in Welsh churches to address the Conference. Many speakers at the Conference were men of great ability. In the nineteenth century the ministry still attracted a large proportion of the ablest young men in Wales. College photographs of students at Bala and Trevecka show a substantial proportion of all the Welshmen who had the opportunity of further education. It was not simply filial esteem which led Dr. T. C. Edwards to resign from the Principalship of the University College at Aberystwyth to succeed his father at Bala.[10] The College at Bala was still a large and influential educational centre. Little wonder therefore that many speeches at the Conferences revealed original and penetrating minds, among which were notably those of Principal Owen Prys, Prof. Ellis Edwards, and Dr. Cynddylan Jones.[11] Nor could the English-speaking churches forget that many of them had been founded due to the initiative of Welsh-speaking churches; perhaps the most notable case recorded was at Blaenau Ffestiniog where over forty quarrymen had each given £5 to help in the founding of an English-speaking church. By 1897 there were 229 churches which were English-speaking and which had 124 pastors.

The Conferences were held to stimulate the work of these churches. It was not long before some speakers felt that the worth of the Conferences was diminished by the absence of any legislative authority and had become an occasion for ineffectual verbosity. Some, however, such as Rev. Edward Parry, Newtown, held that it was an advantage to be free of the drudgery of legislation (1908, 26). However, the Associations were not without understanding of the difficulties of those who spoke only English and they began to arrange special joint sessions of the Associations to coincide with the Conferences and at which English-speaking ordinands were ordained. The first ordination of this type was in 1895 and was described by *Y Goleuad* as an occasion never to be forgotten.[12] Moreover, in the nineteen-thirties an English Churches Council was set up by the Associations which was aimed at dealing with issues specially vital to the English churches. However, such steps led to requests for the setting up of an English Association with full legislative power. In 1931, Rev. R. L. Powell, Wirral, said such an Association would allow for more adequate treatment of the needs of English-speaking people and would give to ministers who spoke only English the opportunity to take part in administration. This point was reiterated by Mr. J. Mortimer Harris, Chester, who said that the existing predominance of Welsh influence in the Church made English-speaking members feel inferior and thus their loyalty was strained. Harris felt that this was one of the reasons which discouraged recruitment for the ministry and accelerated the departure of ministers to other spheres of labour (1931, 33-7). Harris also held that since the Welsh churches were to be found mainly in areas where they had been long established their outlook was not geared to the needs of the English-speaking areas. The policy of the Associations was marked by proverbial Welsh caution and did not meet the needs in seething industrial areas (1931, 38). Rev. G. Parry Williams spoke for the Association in the North at the 1932 Conference and admitted that the English churches were the progressive churches of the Connexion and even though these churches had gained some members from the Welsh churches he nevertheless rejoiced in the strengthening of the Church as a whole. Rev. J. D. Evans, M.A., Moderator of Association in the South, however, claimed that the Welsh section of the Church was the senior partner and he went on to discourage aspirations for an English Association which he held would further fragment the Church. With great promptness the Rev.

J. L. Jenkins, Llanelli, protested against the propaganda in the preceding speeches. The Conference decided to ask the Associations to include in a forthcoming Bill to be presented to Parliament provision for the formation of an English Association, and also that in the meantime the Conference should be given the right to make nominations for the membership of the joint Council of the Associations which was charged to attend to matters of special interest to the English churches. Rev. J. M. Jones, M.A., Merthyr,[13] and Rev. George Thomas, held that this Committee was a device to delay the setting up of an English Association which was urgently needed as an answer to the frustration of the monoglots (1932, 38-44). The weight of the Conference was on the side of caution and the wisdom of this attitude was proved in 1933 when it was shown that the Presbyteries in both Associations were about equally divided on the need for an English Association (1933, 39). Moreover, in 1935, Rev. J. D. Evans, who was then Moderator of the General Assembly, sent a message to the Conference discouraging the emergence of an English Association and stating that in their present state as a Conference they "were not doomed to spend weary laborious days in the arid desert of resolutions" (1935, 53).

However, if some events tended to point to the separate life and policy of the English-speaking churches, the Conference was never unmindful of links with the Connexion as a whole and with the wider family in the World Presbyterian Alliance. Of course, it was realised that the Welsh Presbyterian Church was a member of the Alliance but with a difference. It had its own ethos and structure which arose from its origins. Some were more eager than others to stress the points of accord and to hold that the name of "presbyter" was a New Testament word well-suited to express the long inheritance of the Church and therefore more suitable than the more recent and sectional name of Methodist. Principal T. C. Edwards brought his great prestige to the defence of the Methodist name as the basic feature of the Connexion ; for him Presbyterian features were incidental and secondary. This was somewhat unexpected in the son of so keen an advocate of Presbyterianism as Lewis Edwards. Dr. T. C. Edwards' brother, Rev. D. C. Edwards, Merthyr Tydvil, spoke at the second Conference in 1892 at Liverpool and he took a very pragmatic line and desired the best of both elements balanced in the Connexion. He held that Presbyterianism was a form of government calculated to secure the liberty of the subject and conserve the interest of the community as a whole ; it was the golden mean between Episcopacy and Independency. It also preserved the parity of ministers and combined the churches in representative courts. Unlike other forms of Presbyterianism the council of elders had no statutory powers in Welsh Presbyterianism wherein the congregation, met together as a seiat, was its own basic court and had much autonomy over against the presbyteries, associations and General Assembly. Edwards did not claim that Presbyterianism was the only form of government authorised by God but he held that it had been justified by practical experience. He agreed with Lightfoot on the essential identity of presbyters and bishops in the New Testament but did not hold that this prevented further development if occasion required it. He also held that the various courts of the Connexion were a valuable means of avoiding "what I consider the greatest of all apostacies, the gradual development of sacerdotalism" (1892, 6-8). He concluded by saying that while the form of the Connexion was a form of Presbyterianism its soul and spirit and distinctive characteristic was its Methodism (1892, 8).

Rev. R. H. Morgan,[14] a minister with a gift of trenchant speech which he used zealously in the cause of the Disestablishment of Anglicanism in Wales, had no hesitation in claiming that Presbyterianism had found a means of combining firm doctrines with an effective constitution ; he claimed that Anglicans had satisfactory doctrine but an ineffecive constitution while the Salvation Army had a strong constitution but chaotic doctrinal activity which amounted to belief in loud activity and in General Booth. Welsh Calvinistic Methodism escaped these extremes. By nature the Welsh were full of emotion and sentiment but because of the Calvinist influence they were not so fickle as the Irish and French. Calvinism might have overstated some points and some of its asperities needed to be toned down but it had preserved the Welsh from presuming upon God (1892, 9-12). Not unexpectedly the remarks on the Salvation Army drew some protests ; Rev. John Roberts, Chester, said the Army had only one aim, namely, "Come to Christ" (1892, 13).

Dr. T. C. Edwards sailed into the debate with all the Methodist flags flying. He gave one of the most unusual definitions of Presbyterianism and persisted in it even when challenged by Rev. R. H. Morgan (1892, 16). Dr. Edwards said that wherever men united for common action and to resist one man's assumption of authority there was a form of Presbyterianism ; on this basis he could say there were Presbyterian

Wesleyans, Presbyterian Arminians and Presbyterian Lutherans. Moreover, wherever men united for action their aim was to consolidate and define their position but this, in Dr. Edwards' view, was not the Church's basic work. That work was to save the world and the Presbyterian Church of Wales could best do that by stressing its Methodist ancestry. He was not enthusiastic about union with the Presbyterian Church of England ; "life and warmth is preferable to formal unions with any denomination". He said he could only countenance union with the Presbyterian Church of England if it had the Methodist spirit ; he saw no need to sacrifice the Methodist heritage for the sake of a name "which stresses government rather than the highest aim of the spirit" (1892, 14). Rev. Edward Parry was later to show in his presidential address that he was a true son of Methodism but in 1892 he claimed that the integrated system of Presbyterianism had proved its practical value in protecting small congregations against rapacious landlords. (1892, 16).

Dr. Cynddylan Jones raised the issue in his presidential address in 1895 and he differed considerably from the views of Dr. T. C. Edwards. He held that Calvinism was not something peculiar to Presbyterianism since there were Anglicans, Baptists and Independents who held Calvinist doctrines. Methodism was also a temporary and accidental title. Dr. Jones held that Presbyterianism would be the name which would eventually prevail since it was "etymologically right, ecclesiastically proper, and scripturally true". It linked the Connexion with the world-wide Presbyterian family and suited the divine purpose to set the solitary in families" (1895, 42-3).

In 1909 Rev. J. Glyn Davies, the retiring President, spoke in defence of the title "Calvinistic Methodism". In its Calvinism the Connexion witnessed to the splendours of God, and in its Methodism it witnessed to roots which were neither Baptist, Congregational nor English Presbyterian (1909, 24).

Many speakers were also aware of the weaknesses of Presbyterianism. Abuses could creep in and the organisation was largely dependent on the quality of those who held office therein. Rev. J. R. Hughes, Tonypandy, said that "when Deacondom or Committeedom descends to intolerant domination it is as objectionable as papal councils" (1896, 47). The danger of such abuses has been the staple fare of novelists and journalists for many decades. In 1903 Principal Prys deplored the narrow and limited outlook of provincially-minded men who often held power in the churches (1903, 26), but Rev. Edward Parry, Newtown, defended Welsh provincialism and said that Welsh Presbyterianism should go its own way simply because "we want to go our own way" (1908, 25-6).

When Rev. John Roberts, M.A., Cardiff, addressed the Conference in 1934 he revealed a mind of rare vision and capacity. He had no hesitation in probing the weaknesses of the Connexion and among these he counted the tendency to provincialism. The Calvinistic Methodist movement had begun among the Welsh and had won great trophies among them, but "the Welshman of all ages, sanctified or unsanctified, has more race consciousness than any other creature God ever made". Compared with John Wesley who made the world his parish Wales was "the Welshman's parish and his world and it was only the grace of God which took the Welsh missionaries to the Khasia Hills in India". Nevertheless, great things had been achieved in Wales. Tremendous preaching and the singing of William Williams' great songs of vanquished doubt and fear had been factors in the growth of the movement. Moreover, the message had been a religious message and had been free from moralistic obsessions with particular sins. The movement had not been linked with a particular party and so had avoided the twilight which had fallen on the Connexion in the twentieth century due to its links with the Liberal Party. The movement had also been fostered by an "unbroken succession" of leaders in local areas, often in lonely places. Also, as well as the great preachers, there were the hosts of nameless men whose work had been vital for the survival of the Connexion and it was often from lonely outposts with their few and scattered members that there came some of the greatest leaders. Roberts also went on to deal with the future prospects of the Church. Its resources were limited. It did not claim to be a national Church since there were regions where it counted for little. Nevertheless, it had in 1934 183,044 members and though this was lower than a decade earlier yet the Connexion would still be a sizeable body in 2000 A.D. even if the decline continued at the rate of one thousand each year. Moreover, most societies had had a thin time since 1926 and depopulation was an aggravating factor. The movement had been in existence for two hundred years but this was not much in the roll of the centuries and was no guarantee of immortality. Many had looked to Llangeitho as their Jerusalem for two hundred years but many had also looked to Ystrad Fflur for four hundred years before Rowland began his work at Llangeitho, and for all the faults and frailities of the monks Ystrad Fflur had been a "centre of light in dark days and a well of life in a dusty land". None could tell whether or not Llangeitho would go the way of Ystrad Fflur or stand for another two hundred years. The monasteries had been dissolved because they had ceased to satisfy or soothe the spirit of man and "we shall live and prosper as long, and only as long, as we meet the needs of men, their deepest and highest needs" (1934, 46-51).

Rev. D. O. Calvin Thomas, M.A., Aberdare, followed with an address on the mission of the Church in the world and in Wales. The whole Church existed to show forth the glory of God and to win the world to live in the light of that glory and the special contribution of the Presbyterian Church was the kindling of enthusiasm. Order and sacraments were perhaps not sufficient to justify the continued existence of the Presbyterian Church as a separate denomination but there was an enthusiastic austerity written into the Rules of Discipline which was, in Thomas's view, of vital importance. For example, there was the rule urging family worship, but he thought the neglect of this rule in scores of Calvinistic Methodist homes was a serious loss which had led to their complete secularisation. There was also a rule requiring reverence for the Lord's Day, but in many homes it was customary to devote the day to odd jobs and pleasure seeking. The only remedy for this decline was a renewed enthusiasm and passion for souls (1934, 73-5)

However, behind all the exposition of the foundation principles of the Connexion the daily founding and maintenance and staffing of the local churches went on amid many practical adversities. The growth of English-speaking churches had been begun in most cases by people from the local Welsh churches and had then been fostered by the Home Mission Societies. The North Wales Society had begun its work in 1813 and had founded many causes which eventually became self-supporting. Many churches still depended upon the Society. Rev. J. Calvin Thomas, Hoylake, reported in 1893 that during the previous year £1724 had been paid out to thirty-two mission stations of which fourteen were English-speaking. The South Wales Society had been founded in 1819 by Rev. David Charles, brother of Thomas Charles of Bala, and it had concentrated on Radnorshire where the fifteen societies founded by Howell Harris had withered away. In 1892 the Society had supported sixty-three stations to the tune of £852. Calvin Thomas criticised the Association in the South which at its Aberystwyth meeting in 1883 had recommended that no aid should be given to causes not likely to become self-supporting ; this, in his view, was not the true missionary spirit. He said that the twenty-one churches in the Montgomery and Salop Presbytery were weak and had only 916 members and they could not survive without assistance, yet it would be wrong to withdraw aid from them since their contributions to the central funds were more than £2 for each member which was 6/- above the Connexional average. Moreover, future growth was unpredictable and ventures of faith had to be taken. The Lancashire and Cheshire Presbytery was made up of small churches which had almost all been started with Home Mission help and the membership had grown from 696 in 1869 to 2512 in 1889 (1893, 7-9).

Moreover, the moulding of new causes into churches with settled pastors proved to be a formidable task. Indeed, many ministers preferred the itinerant system to a system which restricted their movements. Congregations were also slow to provide for the upkeep of a settled ministry or to support the Sustentation Fund. Mr. Daniel Lloyd, Walton, spoke in 1893 of the need for "systematic and proportionate giving" (1893, 23). The need had been set out in detail in the first Conference by Mr. William Jones, Newport, who said that the average contribution of members in 1888 to the sustentation Fund had been 21/- each ; some had risen far above this ; other churches had fallen far short, one reaching only an average of 7/6 for each member. If all churches had given 21/- for each member many problems would have been solved ; if all had risen to the level of the best then the total income from the English-speaking churches would have been doubled (1889, 41).

Jones went on to criticise some ministers for failing to be pastors of their people ; he said they only conducted a weeknight service and visited the sick ; they paid social calls if invited but did little systematic pastoral work among the people ; it was a common complaint that "they spend much of their time in comparative ease and idleness which develops into sheer laziness and the ruin of mental and spiritual energies" (1889, 41). He suggested there ought to be greater care in the selection and training of ministers ; in their probationary period they ought to conduct services without receiving any fee because this would be a proof of their vocation. They should also have to spend some time as assistant pastors and then be expected to remain in their first pastorate for a period of from five to seven years. This would curb the early growth of restlessness in the minister himself and would also avoid the frequent disturbance of the life of the churches. He thought that the Wesleyan experience of itineracy had not proved to be sufficiently beneficial to warrant the adoption of a system of regular triennial or quadrennial changes of ministers (1889, 39 & 44). In 1902 Mr. Augustus Lewis, Swansea, spoke of the straitened resources of the Church ; he assailed the "ready-reckoning and vulgar-fractioning class of church office-bearer" who will boast of his shrewdness in getting a preacher in the cheapest market at the lowest possible terms (1902, 50).

The financial weaknesses of the Connexion were stressed by Rev. T. G. Owen in his retiring presidential address in 1912. He noted the rise in the number of graduates among the ministers and he said there was great need to improve the payment which they received. The average yearly income was between £80 and £100, but if ministers chose to go to the Presbyterian Church of England they would find that their income would rise into the range between £400 and £1000. He refused to believe that the Connexion could not do better, scores of members were in the £500 to £5000 income group, and there were some who could give £1,000,000 and still have more than most other members of the Church. He commended the Davies family of Llandinam for their support of the campaign against Tuberculosis and for their gift of £50,000 to the Forward Movement, but there were others who could emulate them if they were so minded (1912, 30-32).

Despite difficulties, the English-speaking churches were in the early years of the century the most rapidly growing section of the Connexion. Rev. J. Glyn Davies, the retiring President, said in 1909 that in the previous decade the English-speaking churches had increased by 31% from 239 to 315, while the Welsh-speaking churches had only increased by 3% from 1098 to 1134 ; also, at the beginning of the same decade the membership of the English-speaking churches had been one ninth of the total membership of the Connexion but during the decade it had risen to one sixth and now comprised 27,540 members (1909, 26-7).

The 1910 Conference was the twenty-first Conference and provided an opportunity to survey the development of the English-speaking churches and this was thoroughly done by the retiring President, Alderman S. N. Jones, J.P., a keen statistician. Between 1888 and 1910 the number of churches in the English-speaking group had risen from

184 to 324, and the number of communicant members from 10,706 to 28,207, and the number of adherents, who though not full members were connected with the churches had risen from 34,086 to 84,303; total collections had risen from £26,220 in 1888 to £63,180 in 1910. However, Jones was convinced that this remarkable rate of increase had been seriously arrested; there had been six new churches in 1909 and 632 new communicants and 1569 fresh adherents, and this was not only less than in previous years but also failed to reflect the increase in the population of the country (1911, 28-9). However, on the basis of his own figures it is doubtful if his depressing conclusion was evident. The average increase of churches, according to his own figures, was seven, and the average rise in communicants was 830 and in adherents 2,391. It is of course true that more recruits might normally have been expected from an increasing membership.

After the passing of almost another decade Mr. John Owens, J.P., Chester, devoted his valedictory address as President in 1919 to a statistical survey of the state of the Church and this was of special interest, coming as it did after the upheaval of the War. Between 1890 and 1918 the number of churches in the Connexion had increased from 1262 to 1486, an increase of 17.7%. This included the English-speaking churches which had increased from 193 to 356, an increase of 84%; the increase in Welsh-speaking churches was 5.7%. The lower rate of increase in Welsh-speaking churches is not surprising as prior to 1890 Welsh-speaking churches had been established all over the country. Over the whole of Wales the number of communicants had increased from 136,051 to 187,834, an increase of 38%, but the increase in the membership of the English-speaking churches from 11,925 to 32,186 was almost exactly 170%; this meant that the increase in Welsh-speaking churches, though substantial, was just over 25%. Adherents or "hearers" had also increased from 290,788 to 326,483, an increase of 12%; in the English-speaking churches the increase was from 12,105 to 42,116, almost 248%; in the Welsh-speaking churches the increase was thus only $2\frac{1}{2}$%. This large group of adherents had originally been drawn from those who had roots in the Established Church but who had moved in the industrial migration to areas where Nonconformist churches were the only available places of worship; this group also came to include those who shrunk from a public profession of faith or who hesitated to conform to the self-denial normally required of members.[15] The existence of this group must have given the Church a large area of contact with a great section of the population. In 1966 the membership of the Connexion has not fallen much below the 1890 figure, but the group classed as adherents has virtually disappeared; this is a serious loss since it means that the Church's life centres around its members and is thus in less and less contact with those on the fringe. In 1919 Owens discerned an even more disturbing trend; in 1918 there had been what might seem a small decline in the number of Sunday School members from 192,806 to 190,825, but, as Owens pointed out, if the trend had reflected the increase in membership since 1890 there would have been 23,000 more in the Sunday schools than there were. Owens rightly perceived that this trend would be painfully reflected in the membership. Owens also pointed out that the 1904-5 Revival had upset any regular pattern of growth. In the two years there had been a phenomenal increase of 29,578 in membership; 5,517 had been lost in the next six years, leaving a nett gain of 24,051; if this abnormal figure were deducted from the total figure for 1890 to 1918 the increase in membership would have been 20% instead of 38%.[16]

Financially, Owens reported considerable increases in both income and debt. Total collections rose from £202,707 in 1890 to £359,090, an increase of 77%. Churches were not afraid to embark upon building schemes and to run up debts which rose from £295,345 in 1890 to £517,554 in 1918, an increase of 75%. Many churches found these debts a heavy millstone in the days of the post-war depression (1919, 7-10). However, Owens was able to report in 1923 that the debt had been reduced from its heavy total by £121,033 (1923, 9).

Owens also reported in 1923 that the membership had remained almost steady since 1919, though the minute decrease of 88 was perhaps a straw in the wind indicating a more drastic decline. Even more serious was the decline of 4,607 in the number of Sunday school scholars and of 9,229 in the number of adherents. These trends had not yet hit the English churches whose membership had risen by 1895 and adherents by 1803 (1923, 7-8).

In 1934 Mr. T. G. Dew, the retiring President, reviewed the state of the Church, not so much from a statistical point of view as from the picture which the Church presented to the outsider. He charged the Church with decadence, carelessness and inconsistency. He saw decadence not so much in any actual decadence but in the constant reiteration of the statement that the Church was decadent and also in a foolish enchantment with an imagined past. He saw carelessness in the lack of reverence for many church buildings compared with the care bestowed by the Church in Wales upon its buildings. Laymen, in his view, did not always do what they could and were often too ready to take offence at trifles ; Dew said he had seen a lot of petty jealousy in the churches.

Ministers, in his view, also gave the impression of carelessness by their frequent inaudibility and light-coloured attire in the pulpit. He saw inconsistency in the fact that many men who prided themselves on their goodness were not averse to shady tactics in business (1934, 15-9).

Rev. R. R. Williams, Chester, returned to the statistical theme in his retiring presidential address in 1935. There were 874 ordained ministers in the Church but after allowing for retired ministers and ministers in other occupations there were just 687 in charge of churches. There were 259 accredited preachers of whom just over 200 were students in various stages of preparation for the ministry. In the 1,500 churches of the Connexion there were 7,612 elders. Membership had declined a further 400 to 182,608 during 1934 but there were still 276,526 adherents though in 1918 there had been 326,483. Out of the 1,500 churches 370 were English-speaking, and out of the total membership 34,787 belonged to the English-speaking churches (1935, 15).

The membership of the English Churches had increased from 8.7% of the total membership of the Connexion in 1810 to 17.13% in 1918 and to 19.05% in 1935. Thus quite apart from their generosity and the quality of their life the English Churches were likely to increase their influence in the Church as a whole.[16]

Chapter II

WORSHIP AND PREACHING

THE weekly services of the Church were its main visible activity and in almost every Conference there were demands for a drastic reform of the Church's forms of worship. In 1889, Rev. John Williams, Chester, spoke of worship as "that reverence, honour and service we give to God, according to His perfect moral greatness"; the human capacity to worship was "an affirmation of our greatness, though we adore in the dust; a proof of our affinity to God, though we are 'unclean'." (1889, 35). He then proceded to outline the current weaknesses in their forms of worship; there was liable to be "unreality, indolence, irreverence, and inconsistency", with no meaning in the reading, no freshness in the prayers, and no heart in the singing; too little power in the pulpit was linked to too much indifference in the pews (1889, 36). He did not advocate the rough, roaring and rousing methods of the Christy Minstrels, but services had to be bright, intelligent, and joyous. He suggested that services should start with a fervent prayer or hymn of praise and should include the antiphonal reading of a Psalm, and he advocated the division of the long prayer into prayers of tolerable length and also the production of an up-to-date hymnal. These refreshing suggestions led up to his final observation that "it is a pity we have separated the idea of worship from the sermon" (1889, 37).

The revitalization of the hymnody of the Church was often stressed, particularly by the musicians who addressed the Conferences from time to time. In 1900 Prof. E. Warren Harding, Mus. Bac., Bangor, addressed the Conference. He spoke of the reasons commonly given for having singing in the services of the Church. Some saw it as an opportunity for a ministerial rest during the service but such a use would be a prostitution of music. Others saw it as a means of giving the congregation something to do, in which case it was little better than a prayer wheel. Others saw it as a means of individual expression or of social fellowship, and with these reasons Harding was in substantial agreement because "I do consider a good emotional hymn to be the best possible preparation for a good sermon". He was emphatic that singing was an activity of the whole congregation rather than of the choir and he found scriptural basis for this in the injunction, "Let all the people praise Thee" (1900, 36). Harding held that Wales had good resources for fine singing due to a good grounding in tonic-solfa ; there were those in many congregations who were able to contribute to four-part singing and he found this superior to the practice which he said prevailed in Holland where men and women were segregated and sang in unison and thus produced strong but monotonous singing. "Yet our congregational singing is not always good" ; this was surely a very moderate criticism perhaps calculated not to close minds to the calculated criticisms which followed. He castigated the lack of attention to expression, the pause at the end of each line even where the sense was impaired, the insensitiveness to a fitting pace, either drawling or racing, the prevalence of faulty enunciation and phrasing. To counteract these weaknesses he suggested there was a need of a good hymn-book, of an efficient organ, and of selecting hymns suited to the changing moods of each service. He advised the inclusion of expression marks in hymn-books, advice ignored in most recent hymn-books on the ground that circumstances demand varying tempos for almost all hymns.

He also advised the wedding of one hymn to one tune so as to avoid the lazy habit of applying one known tune to several hymns of the same metre so as to avoid the trouble of learning new tunes. He admitted that there were exceptions when magnificent words were set to exceptionally difficult tunes in which case a tune suited to the congregation's capacity might be used. Perhaps his most idealistic suggestion was that each congregation should maintain a good supply of tenors and basses who could read an ordinary tune at sight. He ended with the florid requirement of an "artistic and sufficient method by which the congregation can be led or conducted" (1900,37). The comments upon Harding's paper in the subsequent discussion all came from laymen and revealed a wide unrest over the current form of the services of the Church. Mr. John Morgan, Cardiff, was refreshingly critical of many hymns ; if the service was intended to be the worship of God then he questioned the suitability of many well-known hymns. "Hark, hark, my soul", and "O come and mourn with me awhile" were addressed to men rather than to God, and, in his view, if they were to be used they should be read or sung by the minister. Such hymns had been properly used by Sankey as invitations to the people. He also questioned the current mania for the installation of organs and feared it had contributed to the decline of congregational singing; congregations should be able to sing without the accompaniment of an organ, and he saw no reason for the fact that there was as much fuss when an organist failed to turn up as when a preacher broke his publication; at most an organ should provide background support. He was irate at a habit which has happily passed into oblivion whereby an organist would indulge in pedal frolics between each verse of a hymn (1900, 40). Mr. R. D. Evans, Birkenhead, claimed Morgan must have generalised from a rare but admittedly unfortunate misuse of an organ. Mr. T. Ashton Davies, Coedway, lamented that in Coedway there was a great prejudice against chanting, particularly of the Te Deum, and against congregational participation in the Lord's Prayer (1900, 41). However, with all the zest for reform, there does not seem to have been any great desire to introduce chanting.

There had also from early conferences been cautionary notes sounded about the value of more emphasis upon the singing. In 1894 the President, Dr. Ebenezer Davies, had asked how far the lure of music, singing, or even exceptional preaching, had accomplished the conversion of sinners (1894, 30). Mr. Augustus Lewis, Swansea, a future President of the Conference, issued a warning in 1900 against exalting music so as to give the impression that preaching had lost its power to draw sinners who could only be enticed to listen to a sermon if it was sandwished between a trumpet obligato or an organ fugue or a solo rendered by "our leading tenor". He said little would be achieved by whittling worship down to a sacred concert so as to coax people in to take homoeopathic doses of Gospel truths by the promise of a musical performance as a reward for their condescension and patronage. He said he did not mean that proper attention should not be given to making the singing as hearty and confident as possible and he blamed some ministers, "our dear brethren of the cloth", for the hesitant way in which they announced the hymns; it often seemed as if "they felt inclined to apologise to the congregation for having to give voice to the sentiments contained in the stanzas"; congregations also, in his view, had become so painfully proper that he himself often felt he had been guilty of a "serious breach of the proprieties when joining heartily in singing praises unto God"; ministers should encourage the people to join choir and organ "in a tone of decent audibility" (1900 42-3).

In 1903 Rev. E. Rowland, Crickhowell, said that in arranging the Church's worship the needs of the young should be considered. The Church of England had been more sensitive to the changes in taste in art and music and had drawn many young people from other Churches. Instead of condemning these young people for forsaking the Church of their fathers it was more important to seek the reasons for their action and learn therefrom. The revival in ritual and splendour in services in the Church of England was not simply due to sacerdotal pretensions but to changes in artistic taste, and the Presbyterian Church could profit by making its services more attractive, impressive and dignified. Too often, services were stilted and bare (1903, 45).

When Mr. Augustus Lewis gave his valedictory address as President in 1905 he devoted it to a devastating criticism of current practices which was all the more significant coming as it did on the morrow of the 1904 revival. He thought there was room for greater congregational participation in worship and for more guidance from the General Assembly about forms of worship. He was aware of prejudices against liturgy and ritual but he believed there was need for a more adequate framework of worship which would not suppress "rapturous emotional outbursts". In general he preferred tranquil devotions and he was impatient of those antiquated and prejudiced minds which scorned aids to worship but who in daily life were often "high priests of social ritual and legality". Public taste had changed and there was need for more adequate music and more fitting devotions in the services of the Church; he was not advocating the transformation of Sunday evening services into sacred "Pops" where soloists usurped the services or where catchy methods were used which were suited to a cheap-jack or a music-hall manager, nor was he relegating sermons to "microscopic pulpit messages aptly concealed like a medicated powder in a spoonful of jam". As for the music, he would prefer the full orchestra referred to by the Psalmist rather than the organ. There was also a rich heritage of tunes but there were also fresh treasures available from the works of "contemporary devotees worshipping at the shrine of the goddess of music", such as David Jenkins and J. T. Rees. Those who led the worship had also a duty to grow and develop new forms of service but discourses drawn out in a tone sepulchral and dolorously unvaried drove the most insomniac to sleep; preachers sometimes spoke as if addressing the big pew alone and often did not announce the location of the Scripture lesson, a fault which still lingers in some quarters. It was, in Lewis' view, time to offer God more than fog and lassitude and also to inflict upon congregations fewer of "those hue-less rainbows which span the horizon of our services" (1905, 23-8).

Lewis' views drew more support from elders than from ministers which is an interesting comment on the view often expressed by timid ministers that elders would oppose changes in worship. Mr. Jacob Jones, Rhyl, commented that while rejoicing in the Revival it would be impossible to expect the regular routine of worship to be conducted on the same ecstatic level (1905, 29).

Dr. Cynddylan Jones stressed sober simplicity as a mark of Presbyterian worship and felt there was need of restraint in such matters as decoration; the ferns and flowers festooning the Conference platform could suggest that it was a conference of Vegetarians rather than of Presbyterians. Yet simplicity was not the same as bareness; "I cannot but think that our worship in Wales is too bare".

There was, in Dr. Jones' view, need of more dignity in the weekly worship and he urged ministers to procure and use the Book of Order of the Presbyterian Church of England, though with such adaptations as were necessary to suit Welsh circumstances (1905, 62-3). Dr. Jones was eager to experiment along these lines when he was minister of Frederick St. Church, Cardiff, but such forms of service were at that time so uncongenial to the congregation that he was obliged to resign from his pastorate in 1888 though he remained an influential figure and a noted preacher in the Connexion.[1] He was an unconventional genius and at the 1894 Conference he had claimed that he caused a sensation every five years.[2]

In 1908, the President, Rev. J. Glyn Davies, said that while treasuring the freedom of Free Church worship even with its risks of self-advertising vulgarity on the part of ministers he had often winced at some of the prayers he had heard (1908, 86).

Dr. Walford Davies, who was then at Aberystwyth University College and who later was to gain national fame at the Temple Church and on the B.B.C., addressed the Chester Conference in 1919 and spoke of the need for effective singing in the Church. A hymn badly sung had a "positive value to the bad". A hymn was not an item to fill a blank between a lesson and a prayer but was a part of the service in its own right, "a rehearsal for the great concert of praise in heaven". Moreover, men returning after the upheaval of war would not be held by singing which was apathetic, unfruitful or unreal. He felt that in pre-war days singing had become lethargic and there could be no effective recovery without work and he suggested a half-hour of singing prior to and as a preparation for the evening service. He also suggested that congregational singing was impossible if the congregation was scattered among empty pews (1919, 18-21). When he addressed the Conference in 1923 he had by then been knighted. Sir Walford spoke of the combination of reticence and beauty, exuberance and restraint, in good singing (1923, 25-6).

In 1921 Rev. D. M. Rees, Tredegar, painted a very unflattering picture of the Church's worship. The Church was being criticised by "the patronising pressmen and the magazine oracles who mutter wisdom in monthly instalments"; much was made of emptying sanctuaries and gabbling pulpiteers and priestly fanatics. Church members often criticised the careless outsiders but he felt that the question to be asked was why the outsider was not attracted. He laid it down that "the Church gets as much respect as it deserves", and people would come if they found there was anything for which to come; it was useless to announce a banquet if there was nothing to eat and he felt that the loafer from a public-house who dropped into a service would not find a warmth in the welcome, a lift in the singing or a power in the preaching which would induce him to return. People would be repelled by joylessness and disgusted by lovelessness and they would ignore worship which was destitute of awe, rapture and passion. Preaching required these qualities more especially at a time when preachers had necessarily lost their claim to knowledge superior to that of their people; contagious passion was their chief weapon (1921, 36-8).

Critical as were many speeches of the services and preaching to be found in the Church, few would have agreed with Mr. J. Mortimer Harris, Hoylake, who said in 1919 that there had been an excessive stress on sermons, the millions of which had not produced "a conspicuously large number of real Christian personalities" (1919, 23). Successive Conferences listened eagerly to sermons from visiting preachers and from noted Welsh preachers. In 1896, when the Rev. Edwin Williams, Trevecka, was preaching, the congregation was so moved that it broke out in stamping of the feet and Williams had to ask them to refrain (1896, 40). There was never any desire to abandon preaching but there was continual discussion as to how current weaknesses could be eradicated and the standard improved.

No one had a higher regard for preaching than Dr. Cynddylan Jones who was also a caustic critic of the foibles of preachers. In 1893 he lashed out at the prevailing habit of beginning a sermon with a quiet fifteen-minute introduction and then leading up to an amplification of the preacher's oratorical resources ending with a final burst of the "hwyl". Preachers had a duty to make themselves heard. Rowland and Harris had been loud and short and forceful and they would have finished a sermon in the time taken in "the low mumbling voice adopted by many Welsh preachers in the first fifteen or twenty minutes". These preachers mumble in this way so that "they might have wind enough to blow their trumpets long and strong the remaining hour". Indeed, some were so slow that at times there was doubt whether they were moving backwards or forwards. The pulpit was the place for dynamics, not mechanics. Of course, there were individual gifts and capacities ; some strong-voiced men could afford to go at a slow pace which would be ridiculous in men with thin voices ; "elephants may walk, but rabbits must run" (1893, 26-7). Dr. Jones held that the basic need for great preaching was a passion for souls. It was not enough to present flowers of literature to people in danger of the flames of hell, and he advised ministers not to "scatter eau-de-cologne to take away the smell of brimstone". Unless there was a passion for souls preaching tended to become harsh and controversial and to reduce the Bible to a series of insoluble problems. With characteristic gusto he poured scorn on the rash of Welsh commentaries on Paul's Epistle to the Galatians ; Paul must have been a poor writer if it took "six little Welshmen who do not know Greek half as well as Paul did to make his meaning clear". The Bible was "God's revelation to the world, to the farmers and colliers of Glamorganshire and Monmouthshire, and not to professors in Oxford or Cambridge, Bala or Trevecka. There was great need for the preaching of commonsense ; the flowers of poetry were very nice but were not food for hungry souls" (1893, 29-30). Dr. Jones also devoted his presidential address in 1895 to the same subject. During its history the Connexion "had reached greater heights in religion than any, Scotland alone excepted". Leaders such as the monoglot Welshman, John Jones, Talsarn, had been "pre-eminently great in ability, though often with moderate attainments in scholarship", and he thought it was a "shame to the young preachers who will not abundantly avail themselves of the numerous educational opportunities provided for them by the government and the churches", but learning could not compensate for the lack of natural ability; "Give me the old preachers of ability without scholarship rather than the preachers of scholarship without ability". University distinctions would not float their possessors to positions of influence; at first people may judge by university degrees but they would soon judge the degrees by the sermons. The scholarly afflatus blowing from Bala and Trevecka in the past had raised in Wales a people who were "the finest critics of sermons the world ever beheld", and this tradition ought not to be replaced by a generation of weaklings "with the Oxford or Cambridge trademark clearly visible on their polished blades"; sharp sickles were useless in baby hands.

Dr. Jones realised that a great change had come over Wales since the early days of the Methodist movement; indeed it was that movement which was largely responsible for the forward leap in literacy and general education which had made it impossible for ministers to assume that they were speaking to people who had only a minimal knowledge of men and affairs and of general culture. It was, however, "rank nonsense" for ministers to think that they had to keep up with all branches of knowledge and to appear omniscient; it was their duty to be masters in their own field of theology. Such mastery involved the use of imagination which was not the same as extravagant flights of fancy or as rankly luxurious metaphors reminiscent of the African jungle. In practice, congregations were often forced to behold imagination moulting and casting its feathers till the floors of the churches looked thick with down like a barnyard in the moulting season. Dr. Jones said imagination had to be kept within bounds; there ought to be no "unrestrained guesses and extravagant statements"; there ought to be no violation of the laws of thought or of a sound scriptural exegesis but there was ample scope for exploring and bringing out all the undiscovered hues of doctrine. He believed that Welshmen had a special capacity for such work and he envisaged a school of theology at Jesus College, Oxford, or at Aberystwyth, "not as an appendage but as the crown and glory of our national scheme of education" (1895, 42-7).

In 1893 Rev. Thomas Rees, Merthyr, had appealed for a higher valuation of preaching which was not antithetical to worship but was itself an act of worship. He held that some Anglicans had devalued preaching but the result was a growth in the grotesque mummeries of ritualism. He also saw in the growing habit of calling men to a definite pastorate a threat to preaching for men were likely to be called for reasons other than ability to preach. Search would be made for men with affability and cheerfulness and the gift of being free with people and mixing with them so as to draw them to Church but the effort would be in vain if the minister could not preach to them once they were in. Good preaching would compensate for many other faults even for great drawbacks as a visitor. The New Testament gave a basic commission to proclaim the Gospel (1893, 33-6).

Rev. Seth Joshua, the notable Forward Movement evangelist, was not much enamoured with developments towards liturgical care and propriety nor with the growing interest in architecture and organs. In his eyes, the wearing of gowns in pulpits was a strutting forth in petticoats. Nor was he much cheered by the growing number of graduates in the ministry; he said they would soon be "as plentiful as potatoes in Ireland,—I beg their pardon—, as numerous as stars in the firmanent" (1901, 81).

In 1909 Rev. J. Morgan Jones, minister of Pembroke Terrace Church in Cardiff and later to become Superintendent of the Forward Movement and an LL.D. of the University of Wales, called for zeal and clarity in preaching. In his view, respectability in conduct and elaboration in buildings could repel "the man in fustian". He said there was great gain in having a learned ministry but there must not be any loss in zeal to go to the man in the street or to express the old truths in forms intelligible to the masses; in any case, the "profoundest thinkers are always clearest" (1909, 64-8).

In 1908 Rev. Edward Parry, M.A., Newton, spoke against any downgrading of preaching; ministers should keep a clock at home to ensure their timely arrival at the chapel but there should be no clock in the chapel lest it might suggest that the time for preaching was limited (1908, 27).

In 1920 Rev. R. R. Roberts, a past President of the Conference, delivered an address which was notable not only as the product of a highly original mind but also as an assessment of the place of preaching after the Great War. Compared with "our fathers who knew exactly where they were, always", Roberts held that we had become bereft of an incisive, definite and final note. This was not altogether a weakness since preachers had often been far more sure than it was possible for men to be. Vast new worlds of thought had opened up, and biblical criticism and historical study made it impossible now to "bludgeon and slaughter an opponent with the ipissima verba of Scripture". The Bible was now seen with a perspective and proportion, and with a scale and graduated value leading ultimately to Christ. This made the Bible a more living book but it could not be quoted so decisively as of old. Spurgeon's method of quotation was arbitrary and unscrupulous though his outlook was redeemed by its Christocentricity. Roberts said that the Church could no longer make absolute pronouncements upon every problem, but he also held that the vital elements of Christianity would emerge more clearly than ever out of the current confusion. One lesson already learned was the need to make Christ central for the Bible, Church and Tradition. Even this measurement was not easily applied since the mind of Christ was not always easily discerned. Christ's mind was so great that human estimates thereof must undergo continual revision. However, there was an immovable bedrock in the moral greatness and loveliness of Jesus Christ, and face to face with that there was room for a healthy dogmatism. Indeed, when the new vision of Christ was followed by a new reconciliation in the heart the preacher could do no other than dogmatise. Dogmatism had fallen into disfavour so much so that "no well-groomed man in the congregation shall go out feeling himself a miserable damned sinner". However mistaken the views of bygone preachers they could instil the fear of God and show how different was the Christian way from current secular ideas. Unless it was different there was not much point in going to Church. Roberts thought that the Keswick movement for all its eccentricities was to be admired for its insistence on the distinctiveness of the Christian life (1920, 18-23).

In 1930 Rev. D. M. Rees, whose forceful criticism of current forms of service has already been noted, spoke of the preacher's task; he had to be a modern man while applying an ancient and changeless Gospel to changing needs. Moreover, there was a gap between minister and people. The average minister unconsciously used a vocabulary of 2000 words but the uneducated man had only a basic 500 words. Moreover, education tended to focus ministerial interest on the cogency of argument, but truth without emotion never kindled faith. Jesus was thought to be beside himself and Paul was dubbed as mad. Rees held the general view that the passionate appeal was about all that was left to the preacher. A contagious passion for souls must not be replaced by socialism, science, philosophy, literature, sensationalism or anecdotes.

He advised ministers to preach the simple positive truths; "Burn your chaff in the private threshing floors of your own soul" (1930, 39-43). Rev. John Edwards, the retiring President, spoke in 1931 of preaching as one of the most effective means of counteracting indifference and materialism and the anti-Christian spirit of the age. It was also the means of offering the gift of God (1931, 21). Prof. T. A. Levi, Aberystwyth, put up an unqualified defence of preaching in 1935; he said no man was ever converted except by a sermon, and preaching was more important than any sacrament (1935, 43-4).

Rev. G. Humphrey Evans, Moserah, said that preaching was important but had been debased in Wales where a preacher was not esteemed for the truth of his material but rather for his appearance, oratory and gestures. People pandered to the preachers' vanity by treating them as performers. Evans quoted Lloyd George's verdict that among the Welsh "to listen to fine preaching and to criticise the preacher is their form of recreation". He also quoted a drastic little book entitled, *The Welsh Pulpit*, which said that such features as having two preachers at big meetings brought out the worst features in human nature and tended to "pamper the preachers' lust for fame and to gratify the people's passion for oratorical displays". Preaching had in Evans view been prostituted to emotional entertainment, mental recreation and the raising of funds. He suggested that the real test of belief in the efficacy of preaching would be seen if church members would give up their seats, and if need be stay out of the big meetings so that outsiders could get in to hear. Such members would of course contribute generously so that there would be no need to have a collection at such services. Unlike Prof. Levi, Evans welcomed the recent emphasis on the link between preaching and the Communion. This ought at least to make clear that when at last the people understood Jesus' message they crucified him. A highly praised sermon was not necessarily near to the Gospel. Indeed it was fatal to trim the message so as to win immediate applause. Ministers had been criticised for not being practical in their guidance but when they had tried to be they found they were criticised for not preaching the Gospel, but this criticism emerged from the kingdom of darkness which loved to keep preaching in the clouds and devoid of intellectual content. Preaching which emphasised individual salvation did not always produce people noted for Christlike living. As a technical addendum,

Evans advised ministers to abandon dull and slow preaching (1935, 47-51).

Early in the twentieth century there were occasional alarms about future recruitment for the ministry. There were an increasing number of useful professional openings and there was, according to Rev. J. Glyn Davies, the retiring President in 1909, already a dearth of recruits from among the most brilliant young men in Wales. Davies was also alarmed that few sons of ministers and elders seemed to have heard the call to preach (1909, 25, 28).

In 1922, Rev. S. O. Morgan again lamented the dearth of recruits for the ministry from the families of denominational leaders. Sons of the manse and sons of elders could be found filling other posts of influence but few were entering the ministry. He admitted that the current stipend was less than the average roadman's wage but the ministry still offered unparallelled opportunities in the pulpit, on the platform and in the home (1922, 40-5). In 1923 Mr. John Owens, J.P., said the Church was at a standstill because so many churches had no pastoral care, and he regretted that, unlike Scotland, the sons of the manse were not entering the ministry (1923, 8).

Another feature of Welsh Presbyterianism had been the "Church Meeting" or Seiat, but there were many complaints about the difficulty of sustaining this meeting with any vitality. Prof. Ellis Edwards said these meetings had been a witness to the wholeness of the Church; all members had the opportunity to share in leading in prayer, in explaining the Church's teaching and in administering discipline (1900, 22-3). In 1901 Rev. Barrow Williams deplored the shallowness which had invaded such meetings; prayers had become full of set phrases and misquoted texts; and Rev. J. Glyn Davies said that such meetings now veered between Quakers' meetings and meetings of "twaddle and bare platitudes" (1901, 62-3). Anxiety about the value of these meetings was sharply expressed in 1909. Mr. Edward Carwright, Dowlais, said that business, lectures, concerts, and theatrical performances were drawing away large numbers from the Seiat and he said that if the Seiat was to survive there was need of more zeal, more faithfulness, and more preparation; he even suggested making these meetings into tests of membership by the adoption of attendance cards and the holding of week-day Communion services attendance at which would be required of those wishing to retain their membership (1909, 48-50). Rev. J. Calvin Thomas spoke of the deadening effects of long prayers in the Seiat and he recalled one meeting which lasted one and a half hours and at which there were only three prayers (1909, 52). However, Mr. D. Harris, Llansamlet, thought that the Revival had freshened and improved the quality of the prayers which were offered not only by ministers and deacons but by members generally (1909, 53).

Funerals have been a distinctive feature of Welsh life ; in few other countries has there been the precise mingling of large attendances, exuberant singing, and elaborate panegyrics. Funerals are also occasions for manifesting the closely knit and inter-related nature of Welsh society as is shown in the extensive lists of donors of wreaths which appear in local papers. Nevertheless, the language of eulogy has been so debased by overelaboration that not all eulogies can be taken at their face value. Moreover, the social ritual cannot be entirely taken at its face value and it has been remarked that there is a form of enjoyment in the lacrymose demonstrations. Uneasiness about the significance of funerals was expressed by Mr. Edwin Rees, Cardiff, in 1902 ; he said that at funeral gatherings the minds of mourners were not centred on the person who had died, but the conversation ranged over farms, merchandise and business (1902, 52). It has to be noted, however, that such phenomena revealed a state of society in which religion and its outward forms were closely woven into the daily concerns of the people. The decorum of the private funeral is not all gain, religiously or socially.

The conferences were continually confronted with the problems which still face the Church. It is a sobering reflection that what are often regarded as trenchant criticisms of preaching were being made many decades ago and apparently with equally small effect. Nevertheless, the very fact of such continual criticism shows a regard for the responsibility and privilege involved in leading the worship of God.

Chapter III

THE FAITH OF THE CHURCH

SERMONS naturally suggest the teaching and doctrine which lay at their foundation, and they also reveal the trends of theology in the Church over a period of time. Rev. J. E. Hughes, M.A., Caernarvon, said in 1902 that the great preachers of the Connexion, such as John Elias, John Jones Talsarn, Henry Rees, Lewis Edwards and Owen Thomas, had all preached "the Catholic Faith of all the children of God" (1902, 41). There was abundant evidence of loyalty to the Trinitarian doctrine of God and to the main credal assertions. There were those who thought that loud reiteration of dogmatic formulae was equivalent to effective defence but there were also those who gave serious attention to issues raised by philosophers, historians, and textual scholars. For example, in the very first Conference Principal D. Charles Davies, M.A., Trevecka, took issue with the view of Comte and T. H. Green that Paul was the key figure in the growth of what was traditionally regarded as the Christian Gospel ; they taught that Paul had died to self and risen to a new life of love and then had objectified this as the death and resurrection of Christ ; this process of objectification had been adopted by the writers of the Gospels who transmuted what had originally been subjective feelings into a record of external events and this had been adopted by Christendom as the basis of its faith. Davies held this theory to be quite unproven and said that though the writers of the Gospels were pre-scientific in outlook they were not pre-critical and were quite capable of assessing evidence (1889, 34). Speakers were also aware of the perennial vitality of the old heresies.

The divinity of Christ was central in the thought of most speakers. This could hardly have been otherwise in a Church steeped in the hymns of Williams Pantycelyn. There was also an acute awareness of the need to reassert the humanity of Christ. Rev. William James, Aberdare, spoke at the first Conference about the reality of Christ's human nature which was not absorbed but was rendered "more truly human by the indwelling of the divine" ; "He was a true man and His life was a real human life ; He fought the battles of life exactly as we are obliged to do ; He really knew more when He was twelve years of age than He did when He was twelve months". This growth was not a mere guise assumed by omniscience. There was real limitation, a true self-emptying in order to achieve His purpose on level terms with all men. James was impressed by the thought of Dorner, the German theologian, who held that for all the gulf between God and man there was nevertheless sufficient kinship to enable the human nature to receive the divine. James rejected any idea of pretended ignorance in Christ as morally indefensible. "He was morally incapable of assuming ignorance ; He passed from one stage of life into another exactly as we do, only He was a better man'. Christ's temptations were real ; "it was not a tournament got up for dramatic effect but a real duel . . . ; the battle could not be harder, and the victory could not be more decisive and complete". This growth and struggle did not imply that in Christ the imperfect was struggling to achieve perfection, and he quoted Bruce and Weiss to illustrate his point. He summed up his view in an aphorism not unlike the view of Wesley ; "perfection and progress are not incompatibles". Christ made the perfect response to His Father at each stage of His life, and James thought that it was not improbable that in glory Jesus was rising to new heights of perfection (1889, 5-9). The centrality of Christ for all genuine Christian thinking was stressed by Dr. Cynddylan Jones who urged all preachers to be sure that all texts were so expounded as to lead to Christ. St. Paul had been blinded by the glory of Christ whom he had met on the Damascus road, and just as Sir Isaac Newton, after looking at the sun, had for days seen nothing else but the glare of the sun so St. Paul, after seeing Christ, had for the rest of his life seen everything in the light of Christ. For this reason Dr. Jones preferred the Christocentric commentaries of Matthew Henry and Thomas Scott to the German critics and their English imitators who "strove to empty every Psalm and every prophecy of Christ" ; where a choice had to be made, Dr. Jones said it was wiser to trust the devout Christian instinct than the niceties of scholarship and the rules of syntax (1893, 30).

Rev. W. Sylvanus Jones, Abergavenny, said in 1894 that some briefless barrister had recently stated that there were scores of young men in Wales who accepted what scientists said, and also that in the churches themselves there were many men who were virtually Unitarians, if not materialists. It is not clear what evidence there was for this assertion, but Jones held that he could not believe in the "salvation of any man who does not accept the Deity of Christ" (1894, 43).

Alderman J. Jones Griffiths, Tonypandy, paid tribute to the practical impact of a true conception of Christ's exalted and universal power ; the Christian was immeasurably indebted to Christ and this was a grand incentive to the performance of Christian and all other duties (1894, 81).

Rev. Thomas Gray, Birkenhead, laid great emphasis upon the importance of Christ for a proper understanding of the Old Testament. Without Christ the Old Testament became valueless for the Christian, and its history was myth, its facts fables, its types meaningless. Christ gave life to its history, realisation to its facts, and substance to its types. However, although he claimed that there was illumination to be gained from every part of the Old Testament by relating it to Christ, yet there was something far-fetched in his discerning of Christ in the description of the Sun as standing still (1930, 31).

In 1909 Prof. J. Young Evans, Aberystwyth, gave a clear account of current thinking on the person of Christ. There had been a reaction against the sceptical minimising of the uniqueness of Christ. He quoted Harnack in support of the substantial historicity of the Gospels and declared that "the Gospels were not written to adapt the life of Christ to the deification of Jesus by Paul". He said that those who could not accept the narratives of the Virgin Birth and of the Resurrection as literal accounts of events did not now dismiss them as variations upon heathen legends and subjective visions but saw in them pointers to inscrutable mysteries. Evans thought that the traditional exposition of doctrine was proving to have a fresh cogency and efficacy (1909, 38-40).

In 1927 Rev. J. J. Thomas, B.A., Cardiff said that they were living in an age intolerant of disputes and impatient of authorities and of claims to infallibility ; even among Protestants the idea of an infallible book "is crumbling away under the critical assaults of modern times", and confidence could only come through a compelling inward authority formed by the Holy Spirit interpreting the teaching of the New Testament as it set forth the person of Christ (1927, 31-6).

The widest variety of thought was found on the doctrine of the Atonement, on what Christ achieved for man, and how He accomplished it. James of Aberdare set forth his view clearly ; "by means of Christ's intense love and sympathy He had identified Himself with the sufferers to such a degree that their sufferings, in some real sense, became His". Christ did a great work but James did not claim to know how He did it; he hides his perplexity under the phrase "in some real sense", but his view was basically that of identification. He hesitated to go so far as to limit Christ's work to His moral influence upon man but he rejected theories such as the "bare imputation theory" which "may satisfy lawyers and jurists but is unsuitable to lead ordinary practical minds unlearned in the law to the great realities of the Atonement". (1889, 10).

Dr. T. C. Edwards discussed the matter in 1892. He admitted that some theories were inadequate; some were even immoral and repugnant to conscience. He also said that the New Testament never spoke of God being reconciled, but he also held, and he quoted Grimm and Meyer in support, that the idea of God being reconciled was deeply embedded in the New Testament and was only rejected by those who held that anger was a passion unworthy of God, "but for my part I cannot conceive of God's being incapable of anger if He is good"; God's love involved hatred of sin and He could not be good unless He hated evil. Edwards then asserted the very positions which have been the source of heart-searching to many. He said that since it was God who sent the Son it would be improper to say that the Son had allayed the divine wrath, but he also said that God ceased from His anger as a consequence of the atonement made by Christ. On the further point concerning the benefit accruing to disciples of Christ, Edwards refuted as immoral any view which held that God treated the innocent Saviour as if he were guilty while treating the sinner as if he were innocent. The sharing in Christ's merits was due to His close identification with men. "Throughout His life He was continually drawing close the bonds that unite Him with humanity; . . . His victory is our victory through the completeness of His self-identification with us". Edwards then asked the further question concerning the means by which Christ drew men into an identification with Himself. He rejected the common view that Christ had procured an abundance of merit by his infinite self-sacrifice. He somewhat unexpectedly followed Bushnell in holding that all owe to God a perfect obedience and therefore Christ's obedience was no more than what was due to God. The key to the sharing in Christ's merits was not to be found in any substitution of his superabundant merits for human sins but in complete identification with Christ. (1892, 21-2).

Prof. Hugh Williams,[1] Bala, who was a noted historian and whose work on the early history of Christianity in Britain is still quoted with respect, stressed the metaphorical nature of such terms as propitiation and ransom. He said that the doctrine of a vicarious satisfaction, if taken literally, was not wide enough to cover all the New Testament teaching (1892, 23).

In 1899 Rev. J. Morgan Jones, Merthyr, said that it was vital to begin any consideration of the significance of the Cross from what Christ Himself did and taught. To start from the Old Testament concepts of law and sacrifice was to place the primary emphasis upon God as the holy and righteous judge, and this led to commercial views of salvation. Starting from Christ, the enquiry was directed towards God as the holy, righteous and merciful Father whose will was the salvation of all His children and whose law is the expression of His righteous will whose motive was love and whose punishments were meant to awaken those He punished to the greatness of that love. Jones rejected any idea that punishment was necessary to satisfy abstract justice. Such a view was, in his opinion, irreconcilable with Christ's doctrine of God; if in the end there were eternally damned souls it would be so in spite of all God's efforts since He took no pleasure in the death of the wicked. Rev. R. J. Rees, M.A., a rising figure in the Conference and in the Connexion, held that Jesus recognised the need of sacrifice to make a propitiation for the world's sin and thus to vindicate the basic holiness and justice of God. Rev. J. M. Saunders, M.A., Swansea, asserted that the message of the Cross of Christ was inseparably linked to the doctrine of a sacrificial, substitutionary death. It was human unawareness of sin and its consequences which made many assert that the objective theory of the Atonement was a repulsive and demoralising dogma. Much of the exegetical ingenuity applied to the Scriptures was, in Saunders' view, an attempt to explain away their plain meaning and was the "veriest cant of intellectualism" (1899, 29-33).

One of the weightiest debates on this issue was the confrontation in 1907 between Dr. Cynddylan Jones and Rev. David Phillips, M.A., who was then a minister in Cardiff. *Y Goleuad* reported that this discussion aroused "immense interest" and, though the majority supported Dr. Jones, the frankness and fearlessness of Phillips "commanded kindliest and general appreciation".[2]

Dr. Jones began his address with the basic assumption that divine love was the original cause of the atonement, that is "the ground of reconciliation or God's reason for extending forgiveness to sinners".

God did not love the world because Christ died for it but Christ died for it because God loved it. There was therefore no room for the cant that God needed to be placated. Grace was God's unmerited love for a guilty world, and the sinner's heart was melted to penitence by the sacrifice of Christ which revealed that love. However, in Dr. Jones' opinion, there was much misunderstanding of what God's love was. For some, such as Bushnell and his admirers, there was an eternal unhappiness in God which led Him to suffer. In the words of G. B. Stevens in his well-known work on the Atonement, "in the work of Christ we behold a transcript of the eternal passion of the heart of God". A. M. Fairbairn had also assailed the doctrine of the impassibility of God. Dr. Jones held that the New Testament did not teach about the agony of God but about the sympathy of God, and sympathetic as He was he did not look alike upon the sinner and the saint. Nor could Christ's death be looked upon as an illustration of the natural law of self-sacrifice ; nature had no self to sacrifice. Even in the animal world the mother defending her young did not die willingly. Moreover, in nature the lower forms of life perished to enable the higher to survive ; on Calvary the highest was forfeited for the sake of the lower.

Dr. Jones also dealt with the view that God had no difficulty in forgiving. The difficulty, according to this view, was in breaking down man's obstinacy so that he might accept forgiveness. There was a measure of truth in this view but it was not deep enough to take into account the necessity for God to deal with the terrible reality of sin which had upset the balance of life. Dr. Jones thought that while the old Puritans overemphasised the demands of righteousness the new Keswick emphasis reduced God to a being of infinite softness. If God could save by a mere declaration of intent then surely it was the direst cruelty to deliver Jesus Christ to the shame and ignominy of death.

Dr. Jones' exposition was not altogether convincing. His insistence on the need to restore the disturbed balance did not altogether avoid the dangers which he clearly saw in some substitutionary views. His aspersion on the Keswick mentality was not justified since most Keswick thought has given a large place to the vicarious efficacy of the sacrifice of Christ. Moreover, he was almost too neat in his solution of the Calvinist-Arminian tension ; he said that all believers would be saved for all believers were the elect. He said that there was a doctrine of election in Calvinism with its stress on the electing grace of God, and also in Arminianism with its emphasis upon the possibility of man choosing to remain in unbelief (1907, 29-35).

Rev. David Phillips, M.A., then minister of Frederick St. Chruch in Cardiff and later to be a very influential professor at Bala, began his exposition from human experience and from the commands given by Jesus to his disciples. Jesus taught his disciples to forgive without limit and to do the utmost to bring the offender to penitence. Jesus exhorted his disciples to forgive on the sole ground of repentance. Phillips then held that God had acted on the same principles; indeed, Jesus taught that God forgave. In answer to those who held that God's ways were not human ways and that God must preserve the moral order by just retribution Phillips held that retribution by itself was not ethical but only added suffering and evil to evil. The only thing which could satisfy righteousness was the reformation of the sinner and that reform began with penitence. Phillips went even further and said he could not see any necessity to justify God's forgiveness; it was an act which justified itself. The costly thing for God was not to forgive but to win the sinner. It was this identification with sinners which cost so much and which God alone could undertake. Phillips then expanded the view which had been trounced by Dr. Jones that human sins crucify Christ afresh and cause God to suffer in His people (1907, 36-39).

The doctrine of the Atonement was considered afresh in 1922 and the discussion revealed similar tensions as in 1907. Rev. Emlyn James, B.D., Liskard, said that the central fact lay in God's action to reconcile the world. Since God was absolutely Christlike His activity could not be considered basically on legal lines as though God had to be just but might be merciful. Traditional theories were too much concerned with ideas of retribution and vindictive punishment which did not and were not expected to do the sinner any good. James held there was too much stress on a substitute coming between God and man in a legal sense but "Thank God, much of this teaching is now dead". Of course the wrath of God was a fact; the universe proclaimed it, but it was intended as a way of chastisement and discipline since God's laws serve His ultimate purpose of redemption (1922, 21-25).

James was followed by Rev. Bayley Roberts, M.A., Oswestry, who ridiculed the "Modernist School" as represented by Dr. Hastings Rashdall whom he classed as a good philosopher but as a discredited theologian who had reduced God to a being of infinite softness and who had unjustifiably exalted the parable of the Prodigal Son as though it contained the whole Gospel when in fact it was intended to illustrate no more than the fact of God's joy in finding the lost. Roberts also said that those who defended the doctrine of a vicarious Atonement were more concerned with the generosity of Christ's sacrifice than with the appeasment of God's wrath (1922, 36-8).

Reconciliation between God and man, however achieved, was also seen to be inextricably and uncomfortably bound up in the New Testament with reconciliation between man and man. Rev. Evan Armstrong, Ebbw Vale, pointed out in 1920 that in the New Testament the Church was a reconciled community and estrangement between believers was unnatural and abnormal. Christ had referred to a man who gave just cause of offence to a fellow-disciple and remained unrepentant; such a man was to be as "an heathen and a publican", but this did not mean, as was often supposed, that such an offender was to be put beyond the pale of reconciliation. Rather, such a person was to be loved as a believer loved the unbelieving world and as he ought to love a heathen and a publican so as to win them. Armstrong said this was a hard path since it meant that one who was in the right must make the move to call forth the transgressor's repentance and not wait in righteous aloofness until the offender made the first move. Forgiveness was costly and often seemed less necessary than retribution which often seemed necessary so as to vindicate the right but which could also be a cloak for the expression of the delusive malignity of the human heart. Armstrong defined Christian love as the readiness to stretch out a hand to enemies in sincere goodwill while refusing to silence the claims of right (1920, 30-2). Rev. J. H. Howard expanded this line of thought to cover the necessary path to reconciliation between classes and nations (1920, 32-4).

In the teaching of the Connexion the Cross of Christ has occupied a central place and even in its hymnology the Cross has overshadowed all other aspects of doctrine. There has been comparatively little emphasis upon the Resurrection, but it was never entirely forgotten. Indeed, though it was not explicitly emphasised, it was always in the background. However, it was brought to the front in 1895 by Rev. J. Puleston Jones, M.A.; Jones was born in 1862 and had become blind at the age of two but this did not prevent him from becoming an

Exhibitioner and Scholar at Balliol College, Oxford, and then gaining a First in Modern History. He became minister of the English Church at Prince's Road, Bangor, in 1888 and remained there until 1894 when he resigned ; in 1895 he became minister of the Welsh Church in Dinorwic and thereafter at Pwllheli and Llanfair Caereinion.[3] His fame as a preacher spread far and wide. In his address on the Resurrection he said that no one had been able to produce "any version of the story which is not really much harder to believe than the plain commonsense version which the Gospels have given", but he also held that "the essense of the whole matter lies in something deeper than the physical marvel" ; the Resurrection was the proof that in God death and resurrection are only two aspects of the same life. "Christ's death is a death which means life" (1895, 14).

The Calvinist strand in the inheritance of the Connexion was not neglected and there were attempts in the Conferences to assess its value. In 1901 Rev. Richard Morris, M.A., B.D., Dolgellau, said that Calvin was a man of lofty ideals ; indeed, it was only a great man who could have aroused so much hatred against himself over so long a period. Many disliked his teaching not simply because it seemed to be oversevere but also because it seemed difficult to reconcile with truth and goodness. Morris said that some Calvinistic teachings would probably have to be discarded but there was within Calvinism an abiding value in its living spirit, its emphasis upon the transcendence and immanence of God, its awareness of the enormity of sin, and in the central position given to Christ (1901, 27-31).

Rev. W. W. Lewis, Carmarthen, acknowledged the paradoxical element in Calvin's teaching. God had the power to bring His plans to pass by the best possible means yet He would not violate the dignity of the individual being ; God ordains whatsoever comes to pass and yet is not the author of sin. Yet in this teaching God was given full glory. Lewis held there was need to give fresh emphasis to the need for seeking the glory of God especially in an age when many concentrated upon improving human environment and in alleviating the consequences of human sin ; "human happiness is not the end for which we are to labour" (1901, 32-3).

Principal Prys spoke in 1903 of the great doctrines shared in common with all Christians ; God sent His Son ; Christ died for us ; God was in Christ reconciling the world ; Christians were saved by faith in Christ ; in Christ was the power of life and as Christ lived so

Christians would live with him. Apart from these central doctrines there were particular doctrines drawn up to meet special needs. Calvinism had permanent elements but had also particular and transient elements. Moreover, it had aspects which appealed to some types of mind just as Arminianism appealed to others. Principal Prys thought that while one could not convert the other both could dwell together in the Church on the basis of commonly-held essentials (1903, 22-4).

The doctrine of Election was one of the aspects of Calvinism which occupied much time at the Conferences and led to many agile attempts to reconcile a doctrine of election with a universal offer of salvation. For example, in 1892 Dr. T. C. Edwards said that while the death of Christ made sure of the salvation of some it also made possible the salvation of all (1892, 22). Prof. Ellis Edwards, speaking at the same conference, said that the doctrine of Election could not be held in the stark form often set forth by their fathers. It was true that man had not the power to save himself but it was also true than man had the power to get that power (1892, 15).

With the passing of the years any stark doctrine of Election became increasingly distasteful and in the years after the Great War there was a tendency to minimise the importance of all theological questions. It was therefore noteworthy when Rev. W. Watkin Williams, Swansea, delivered a profound address in 1927 ; his results, though somewhat unusual, showed the working of a clear mind. He thought that Paul's emphasis upon God's right freely to exercise His grace had been twisted in later thought to present a picture of a God who was not gracious. Augustine's commentary had ousted the softer lines of Origen's teaching, and Williams found it difficult to see how even Hell witnessed to the glory of God. Similarly, he found Calvin's teaching that even the reprobate were a witness to God's glory difficult to sustain. Williams held that God's whole nature must be at work in all His actions, and any view which held that God's grace was irresistible implied a lack of grace in God. He found much satisfaction in John Oman's classic work, *Grace and Personality* ; it showed how gracious was the God whom Jesus revealed. God was neither a celestial Kaiser relentlessly enforcing His will nor a celestial Micawber waiting for something to turn up. Williams said that his own experience of human freedom and God's grace made it impossible for him to accept any determinism, materialistic, economic, or theological, however plausibly stated. He also concluded that if he accepted the doctrine of God as the sovereign Father then he could not accept a doctrine of ultimate reprobation, but was driven to universalism. He found a wonderful Gospel in the news that the Shepherd went out to seek "until he find". Nor did Williams rest content in Von Hugel's explanation that God would be "all in all" when He had subjected all to Himself but he said that Von Hugel had himself been perplexed by the doctrine of Hell since its existence implied that God had not secured complete triumph in the realm of human souls and that He could not save the godless. Williams allowed that these were dark matters but for himself he could not rest in any doctrine which implied a defeated God Who though He willed all to be saved would be unable to accomplish His purpose (1927, 19-25). This theme was taken up by Rev. C. Vincent Williams, M.A., Llanelli, who said that the idea of God's transcendence was an important strand in Christian theology which had been re-asserted by Karl Barth. Paul had indeed asserted the unlimited will of God but recent restatements of the doctrine had minimised the complementary truths of human freedom. Paul had left these differing emphases unharmonised in his teaching, but Calvin and Barth pursued the thought of God's omnipotence to its logical conclusions. There was, however, little point in trying to show that Paul did not teach a doctrine of Election or that it was merely an election to service. Williams held that no doctrine of Election was tenable if it implied that grace was irresistible; grace which was irresistible could not be grace. It was vital to preserve the unity of God; whatever doctrine of Election was taught by Augustine and Aquinas, they both also held that God's character, purpose and power could not be thought of in isolation from His love; even God could not use unworthy means to attain His ends (1927, 26-9).

It was part of Calvinist doctrine that while man may not know the inscrutable decrees of God it was necessary to assume that where the Word of God was proclaimed, Sacraments administered, and discipline exercised, there was the true and visible Church of Christ. This was assumed in many cases without much open discussion of the issue. In 1913 Prof. J. O. Thomas, Bala, admitted that the Connexion had not given much attention to setting forth a doctrine of the Church but he held that this was not a matter of regret since the New Testament did not deal at length with the subject, and even the two references in Matthew's Gospel were probably the outcome of the thought of the early Church. In Thomas' opinion, Christ's teaching was centred on people as individuals, each in his own sphere and each standing as a witness for God and the right (1913, 22-25). Prof. David Williams, Aberystwyth, took a more definite position and held that the idea of the People of God was deeply rooted in the New Testament and had been given specific form by St. Paul in his use of the concepts Bride and Body. The Church was a priestly fellowship bound together in a vital faith but within this unity there was room for variety of creed and organisation. This, of course, savours of that indefinite quality in platform utterances which sounds so satisfactory until an attempt is made to define the limits of variety ; if there are no limits there can hardly be any point in trying to define the Church at all. Williams also spoke of the Church's witness in its worship ; divorced from a worshipping community, preaching was likely to become a display of human wisdom. The witness must also be followed by the witness of the whole life (1913, 26-30).

Never was a higher doctrine set forth than by Prof. Ellis Edwards in his sermon in 1897. He began by postulating that "man is not human until he is divine". Man could only realise his potentiality by dependence upon God who was goodness. Man by nature had more affinity with goodness than with evil and there were always within him stirrings of the divine but "conscience cannot cause itself to be obeyed". Man needed fresh resources of the power of God and this came in answer to prayer and through the Church. The New Testament may not teach that the Church was absolutely necessary as a means to bring men to Christ but the man who only read the Bible without going to any church was nevertheless entering through the Bible into the world of the continuing life of the Church. Moreover, any salvation worthy of the name was salvation into a society. No one could live apart from society ; it required the presence of others to call out the powers of the individual. Further, just as in the scientific field most men were dependent on the vision of pioneers so in the Christian life "we never get beyond the views of particular men". Apostles, Evangelists, enlighten those who read their works. To come to these writings for light was to come to Christ through members of his Church. The promises of God "must be fulfilled in a fellowship or they will be fulfilled in none". Christ had made the Church to be his body and he worked through its members. The Church did not exist for its own sake but for the glory of God and the service of men. It had to tell men what kind of being God was and to live a life corresponding to its message (1897, 80-3).

The doctrine of the Church was raised again in 1923 and was discussed against the background of the common post-war idea that the Church was a dispensable extra and that real Christianity was as likely to be found outside the organised churches as inside them. Prof. David Williams again held that there was a tougher fibre in the New Testament. The Pauline doctrine of the Body was a means of seeing the Church as a society of love and fellowship in the Holy Spirit. Williams believed there was a legitimate place for such terms as the extension of the Incarnation and even more for the extension of the Atonement when thinking of the life of the Church. Moreover, the Church was in some measure a standard for measuring other societies whose purposes could only be properly fulfilled as they subserved higher than mundane ends. This would also break up the bad division between sacred and secular, between so-called Church work and domestic or professional duties. Indeed, the religiosity of religious people was one of the worst enemies of real religion. Williams also held that the Church was both visible and invisible. There was no church at all if there was nothing more than individual Christians but neither could any organisation be unreservedly equated with the true Church (1923, 15-21).

Rev. G. A. Edwards,[4] who was later to become a professor at Bala and Principal at Aberystwyth, covered similar ground. He questioned the assumption that there was a churchless Christianity outside all churches. There were obviously people of high principle and conduct outside the churches but such people were not what the New Testament meant by Christians. Moreover, the concept of an invisible Church, as commonly defined, was meaningless in any New Testament sense. There was, however, great relevance in the question whether or not any existing church was a legitimate development from New Testament Christianity (1923, 23). Rev. A. Wynne Thomas, Wrexham, adopted a mediating position by holding that it was possible to have a churchless Christian but not a churchless Christianity (1923, 23).

Rev. F. W. Cole, Cardiff, spoke in 1934 of the essential mark of the Church and claimed that this was to be discerned in the quality of the Church's devotion and obedience. Unity by itself could not be the unmistakeable mark of the Church ; a unity among weak churches was no guarantee of vitality. The Church's strength lay in its divine foundation and its glorious history in which victories outnumbered defeats and successes outweighed failures. The Church needed to rescue its catholicity from papal and protestant limitations and to show the true catholicity which was hospitable to all truth and inclusive of all believers (1934, 61-9).

Rev. J. Henry Davies spoke in 1933 of what he regarded as the Church's dilemma. The Church was blamed for its failure to stop war and yet was rebuked when it tried to do so. It was blamed for not settling social and economic problems and yet was told it was incompetent to interfere. Its teachings had often been too dogmatic but now they had become too indefinite. It was difficult to discern the Church's proper role but if it was even approximating to its duty its role was not likely to be a safe one (1933, 56-9).

Principal H. Harris Hughes,[5] Aberystwyth, provided a careful review of the doctrine of the Church which was hammered out at the time of the Reformation. The Reformers knew the risks they were taking by their actions. They knew that all schism most assuredly was sin. They knew that the defective Church of their day was still under God's control and that within it there was a measure of security and stability. Principal Hughes saw a parallel in his own situation where there was a fear of a war which would destroy civilization which for all its faults gave a sense of security; to destroy it would be to be left to face a grim future. Yet the Reformers felt they had to go forward because they were under the Will and Providence of God. Such a claim was what was made by every leader from Moses to Hitler and there was great difficulty in distinguishing between the truth of such claims. Moreover, the Reformation had led to widespread and chronic division. In Wales, Anglican and Free Churches were divided, and "for all our profession of brotherhood and talk of reunion" it was clear, in Hughes' opinion, that the forces of secularism and neo-paganism were more united than the Churches. He thought that theology had degenerated into an ideology and he held that this had led to the capitulation of parts of the German Church to Nazi ideology. It was Barth's greatness that he had restored theology to its real task of bringing men to an encounter with the living God (1937, 25-30).

In 1938, amid the deepening twilight before the outbreak of the second World War, Rev. David James, M.A., Newtown, said the Church was the society of those who loved the Lord and was bigger than Presbyterianism or Protestantism and was just then suffering at the hands of pagan forces. In Germany there was a campaign against both Protestants and Roman Catholics, and in Russia Communism wanted to see no church at all. Those who thus tried to trample upon the Church were also noted for their diminishing respect for life and also for a growing callousness to human suffering. There was a great need for Christian unity which was not the same as uniformity in policy, government or creed, since no one branch of the Church had the whole truth. There was need to express the unity which already existed because the Church was already one in Christ (1930, 71-6).

Rev. I. Oswy Davies, M.A., Caernarvon, was one of the few voices in Wales which echoed the message of Barth and spoke of God at work in the Church of Faith, in the fellowship of true believers, as power and truth. In a conference where the tone of many speeches was gloomy Davies spoke of Christ's Kingdom as present in the world as judgement and redemption ; he said that God could use the encircling darkness, as He had done at the Cross, to bring His light to view (1938, 36-40).

One of the most remarkable and most unusual contributions to all the Conference discussions concerning the Church came from Prof. David Phillips who said that the Church was much greater than what was seen on earth. There was a vast membership in heaven and "the other members were looking on from above". Each generation would have to live and die without seeing the world much improved in their day, but as the Church carried on its witness in each age it would gain strength from its "relationship with the heralds above" (1924, 29).

The sacramental teaching of many ministers was unexpectedly high in view of the emphasis given to preaching in the life of the Connexion. For example, Rev. D. C. Edwards, while insisting upon conversion, also made it clear that in his view the precise moment of the beginning of conversion might be beyond the consciousness of any man. The work began at baptism ; "the infant may receive the divine gift of a new life in response to the faith of its parents at the baptismal font ; ... we must hold that the idea of baptism involves the reality of the inward grace of regeneration typified by and accompanying the outward sign of washing in order for it to be sacramentally complete". Thus, there was no ground for assuming that those in the Churches who had undergone no sudden upheaval were not converted. On the other hand, while God could not be bound, outward manifestations could be more hysterical than spiritual. The only true evidence of conversion was further growth into humility, faith and love (1894, 67). Rev. Evan Williams, Abermule, was somewhat less positive but was far from decrying the ordinance of baptism. He repudiated the view that at baptism there was any automatic infusion of grace but even in infant baptism there was a confirmation of the promises of God and he found a warrant for the ordinance in the Old Testament doctrine of the covenant between God and His people (1896, 57-8). Dr. Cynddylan Jones held that the sacramental elements were indeed means of grace and that in the sacraments "heaven touches earth"; he claimed that this mystical doctrine was that taught by the Calvinistic Methodist founders (1896, 66).

Nevertheless, there were too many evidences of the unfruitfulness of infant baptism to allow the unchallenged growth of any belief in automatic regeneration. Rev. J. Calvin Thomas spoke in 1895 of the fact that every fifteen years a generation of the faithful passed away and "a new generation is born with a disposition adverse to the Christian character and discipline ; . . . grace is not hereditary". There was no ground, in his view, for teaching that a supernatural efficacy attended infant baptism so as to make infants indelibly "children of God and inheritors of the Kingdom of Heaven"; "Christ has a new world to save with every generation" (1895, 95).

The Lord's Supper was also frequently discussed and much of the Church's teaching was set forth in the addresses at the Conference Communions. Rev. Evan Williams repudiated any doctrine of the Real Presence such as was set forth in the doctrine of transubstantiation but he held that Christ was present in a very real sense in the Communion service; "we meet around a table, not around a tomb" (1896, 60). Rev. Richard Jones, Mancott, held that because of God's promise the sacramental signs were effective seals of His promises (1896, 61). "God pledges Himself to make His promise good" (1892, 62). Dr. Cynddylan Jones also repudiated any doctrine of Transubstantiation yet held that the elements were more than symbols; "there is some unity, if not identity, between the elements and the blessed Lord". It was his experience that there was "a sacredness and a blessedness to be had at the Lord's Supper that you cannot get anywhere else" (1896, 65-66).

In 1929 Prof. W. D. Davies, M.A., B.D., Aberystwyth, spoke of the meaning of the Lord's Supper but he devoted his time to showing that meaning was an intellectual category and was an abstraction from the reality of the Sacrament which was a communion of personality. The value of such communion was beyond words or meaning. If the subject had to be considered on the basis of verbal definition "no consecration can ever turn bread into anything but bread", but in real life love was notoriously blind. The quest for meaning could dissect and dessicate, yet "the position of faith-experience remains untouched" (1929, 67-70). Rev. John Hughes, Bangor, queried Davies' devaluing of the quest for meaning on the ground that since mind was so vital a part of the human person no explanation could be satisfactory which ignored the claims of the mind (1929, 75).

Rev. Dr. D. Martyn Lloyd-Jones, Aberavon, addressed the Conference on the same topic and with his usual diagnostic precision ruled out five misconceptions of the Sacrament which, though not without a facet of truth, were misleading if exalted to be complete statements of the meaning of the Sacrament. The Sacrament was not a ceremonial calculated to make the recipient feel better, not a commemoration service to recall a farewell supper, nor an occasion for self-examination, nor an occasion for making resolutions for the future, nor a mechanical reception of the body and blood of Christ. The Lord's Supper was Christ's gift of His death and His life to His people. Dr. Lloyd-Jones added a postscript which has been characteristic of his teaching, namely that Christ's death was sufficient "to satisfy God and enable Him to give forgiveness" (1929, 71-74).

The inseparable link between Christian Faith and Morality was never far from the centre of the thought of the Conferences and there was considerable debate as to the basis of morality. Much was made of the danger of over-emphasising morality and making it into a hard censorious legalism. Rev. J. L. Jenkins, Cadoxton, made some penetrating judgements when he said it was easy to fall into a habit of condemnation under the guise of standing for righteousness. He said that "it accords with the conceit of human nature to pose as a denunciator", but redemption was never wrought by Anathemas. It was more important to try to understand the reasons for indifference and hostility to the Church and he discerned one of the main reasons to be the theological habit of making doctrines into matters of speculation and contemplation and so divorcing them from ethics. It was easier to sing, "Heaven is my home", than to make home and society into a heaven. Moreover, he saw in the doctrine of the Incarnation a perpetual spring of ethical impulse and any lasting reform must be rooted in an eternal realm. Therefore, in his view, "Theology must be translated into terms of Sociology" (1902, 33-5).

There were also fears that morality could so easily slip into compliance with convention. In 1904 Rev. Evan Armstrong, Ebbw Vale, accused the Church of being "conventionally pious with pithless push and mawkish fussiness, a thin attenuated prayerless practicalness", and he said the Church was reaping the woeful harvest of soft and self-indulgent complacency which had dulled the edge of conscience. Conscience was "the final tribunal in all human affairs" but it needed to be educated and disciplined because it could either become a bulwark of fossilized morality and crushing formality or a pillar of blatant selfishness. The only reliable conscience was a conscience sensitive to the will of God (1904, 40-1).

Mr. W. R. Evans, LL.B., Ruthin, also analysed the role of conscience as the regulator of dogma. He held that on any showing the person of Christ and His teaching approved themselves to the moral nature of man, even of the man outside the Churches. However, excresences had developed which moral instinct must condemn. Evans held that among dogmas which would not stand scrutiny was "the dogma still supposed to be held by us of eternal punishment", and he found this untenable not because it could not be reconciled with the doctrine of a merciful and loving God but because it was not consistent with the idea of justice. Conscience, in this as in other cases, must be obeyed, and Evans held that a teacher of the Church ought to resign his office if his views became inconsistent with the official position of the Church. Evans did not give any guidance as to how dogmas could be reviewed and, if necessary, revised. He went on to set forth the stark claim that "the man who is misled by his conscience is a better and finer man than the one who has no conscience either to lead or mislead him", and he asserted that the Inquisitor guided by his conscience was a nobler man than the man who simply takes what seems the easy and pleasant way (1904, 440-7). Rev. David Lloyd Jones, M.A.,[6] took Evans to task with characteristic good sense. He said that conscience was a much misused word and quoted the confession of Paul as to the frailty of conscience : "I thought I ought to do many things contrary to the name of Jesus of Nazareth". He also spoke of the conscientious conduct of Catherine de Medici in sanctioning the massacre of St. Bartholemew but this did not make the policy right. On the more parochial level there were those who conscientiously believed it was wrong to go to a non-conformist chapel, and he himself had required twenty years to get rid of the conscientious idea that to indulge in hunting and fishing was proof of ungodliness. Some would say that this was proof that his emancipation was not an enlightenment of conscience. He ended by saying that the only way to get conscience into the right groove was to study Christ (1904, 49-50).

Rev. A. Wynne Thomas, Aberystwyth, returned to the theme of a morality based on convention and he said this was the bane of churches which claimed to be non-conformist; indeed, if a preacher were to be so unconventional as to appear in a white waistcoat he would have to answer for his sartorial waywardness before the monthly-meeting (1904, 52). In 1906 Rev. Tyler Davies, Brecon, spoke of the power of convention which forced "fathers to tread doubtful paths to provide a social standing for their children" (1906, 37).

However, dangerous as was the tendency to use religion to support conventional morality, there was a further danger of separating morality and religion altogether. There were moralists whose outlook seemed to many speakers to be cold and who sought self-mastery rather than to be mastered by Christ. On the other hand, there were some like Rev. J. M. Saunders, M.A., Swansea, who were apprehensive of trends associated with the name of Keswick. Saunders said that the Keswick movement was one of the most potent spiritual movements of the later half of the nineteenth century, but he disliked some manifestations of its spirit which he called a Keswick expression of countenance, a Keswick "cant" which interlarded conversation with such termas as "Dear Jesus", "consecrated", "holy" and "blessed", and which issued from speakers who tended to look down from some towering eminence of experience and of attainment upon other poor creatures. Saunders said that "the true saint of God is the last to know of his own superiority" (1900, 55). It is of interest to note that a recent history of the Keswick movement shows that the leaders of the movement were well aware of these pitfalls and sought to discourage such manifestations.[7]

There were also speakers who warned the Conferences against parochial and comfortable views of the Christian demand. Rev. J. L. Jenkins, Liverpool, said in 1921 that there were multitudes in all congregations who were seeking a safe religion, a religion without risk and which concealed no menace to their habits of ease, their passion for pleasures and their greed of gain. Jenkins said that others perceived the need for campaigning against greed, profiteering and slums but failed to see the need for "all this evangelical stuff about sin and guilt and penitence". He suggested that it was less disturbing to join a crusade against social evils than to tackle the lurking evil within. Both were needed (1921, 29-35). Rev. M. Watcyn Williams, B.A., M.C. Merthyr, said that an understanding of the Gospel involved painful changes in relation to other people. It was impossible to have fellowship with a "man whom you think needs a bath but for whom you will not provide a bathroom". Fellowship was also hindered by latent fears of freedom of which Williams saw proof in "silly resolutions, hysterical condemnations, and attenuated heresy-hunts", but "pressure is vain, fear is folly, anathema mere brutality" (1923, 40-1). Rev. T. C. Jones, Penarth, touched upon the same theme in his valedictory address as President in 1924 when he spoke of the need for the Christianisation of the Church. He said that if the world was to be got into the Church the world must first be got out of the Church. He felt the Church had failed on two counts ; it had stopped making converts and producing saints, and it had failed to restrain the world powers. It also lacked the courage to offend the rich or to disturb the pious who had no concern for a deeper grasp of truth, for generous giving or for social justice. Many in the Church esteemed denominationalism higher than the interest of the Kingdom of God, orthodoxy higher than truth, exclusiveness higher than brotherhood. Salvation involved not only conversion from sin, but also the moralisation of business and the pacification of industry, the purification of politics and the extermination of war. He held that Christianity was enfeebled by the multiplicity of sects of which he calculated there were eleven kinds of Presbyterians, thirteen kinds of Baptists, and seventeen kinds of Methodists (1924, 11-4).

It has been said that one of the reasons for the Reformation was the growing awareness of the contrast between the Church as it was and as it ought to be. There were many Conference speakers who were aware of this contrast in Wales. In 1924 Rev. George Thomas, M.A., Chester, made a scathing attack on the Church and this was all the more remarkable as Thomas was regarded as one of the most immaculate and gentle of men. He said it was a common idea that it was more important to be respectable than to be religious. The respectability of church members was remote from the life of the poor, and when missions were established among the poor they were approached as a foreign people. Church members were angry at "the thriftless waste of those poor whom we despise as failures in the social life". "St. Francis of Assisi with his little brothers would be, of course, intolerable in our pew on a Sunday". Security and stability were the highly prized marks of the middle-class but these were not the marks of disciples. Newspapers nourished middle-class prejudices and painted all other classes in red so that readers felt a glow of righteous anger against all Bolsheviks and would be ready to use inquisitorial methods against atheistic schools and so forget the Cross, the power and wisdom of God. "Safety first is no motive for the Gospel". Even within the Church there was more concern for party spirit, theological problems, and crushing conformity than for true religion. Religion was so abhorrent to many that some sought to escape from such religion as did survive in the churches by joining sects whose basic outlook was the pleasure principle; some went to the Christian Scientists who taught there was no suffering and others to the Spiritualists who taught there was no death, while others went to the Theosophists who saw no need of the Cross (1924, 24-7).

However, these strictures were not taken lying down. Rev. R. G. Jones said thousands in the churches were unmistakeably Christian and the Church had still a glorious future. Prof. David Phillips said there was no easier kind of preaching than exposing the sins of the Church, and he had heard nothing new that day. Evil had been in the world so long that it was difficult for it to take on new forms. Critics of the Church were, in Phillips view, only exposing and criticising themselves (1924, 28-9).

After this survey of the attitude of the Conferences to the traditional doctrines of the Church it is important to discuss how far the Conferences had been influenced by contemporary controversies concerning the composition and authority of the Bible and the relationship between science and religion, and how far, in consequence, it was held that the Connexion was still bound by the dogmatic formulae drawn up and approved in the past.

In the light of later developments it would seem that speakers were often too confident that Christian teaching had emerged victorious and unscathed. Even Principal T. C. Edwards could calmly assert that Christianity was "at the present moment the conquering power" and that the sceptics had suffered a defeat, and he was surely rash in claiming that Huxley had been vanquished by Dean Wace. Though much of Husley's teaching has become outmoded few authorities would allow that Wace was a decisive figure in the controversy (1889, 29). In 1895 the incoming President, Mr. E. J. Baillie, F.L.S., Chester, spoke with similar assurance that "the current philosophies of the time are destroying one another and it is clear that the power of Christianity is the coming power" (1895, 7). Principal D. Charles Davies, Trevecka, was more moderate in his claims when he spoke in 1899. He said many objections to Christianity had been smashed; for example, Paley had refuted the view that the Gospel writers were impostors, Butler had refuted Deism, and Chalmers and Whately had refuted Hume. These verdicts have been substantially sustained by later writers. Davies was well aware of the stormy career of Whately as Archbishop of Dublin, and, though recent study has somewhat improved his standing, there is still much truth in Davies' verdict that "a more extraordinary man than he never sat on the episcopal bench". Davies held that science was "fully justified in dealing with its own observable and measurable fields" but there were other and more important fields and if theologians had often been unwise in circumscribing the scope of science there was also the danger that science could claim too much for itself. However, truth was ultimately one harmonious whole and the supernatural was not at enmity with the natural but only with the unnatural (1809, 30-2).

Many speakers stressed the duty of receiving light from any quarter. Prof. Ellis Edwards was particularly receptive to fresh ideas and was adept at assessing the truth they contained. Prof. Edwin Williams said there could be no warfare between true religion and true science and "the panic in the Church is no credit to its faith" (1899, 23). A similar hospitality of mind was displayed by Rev. D. Lloyd Jones, M.A., Llandinam, whose valedictory presidential address in 1904 surveyed recent trends of thought and gave evidence of a remarkable range of reading. He was a son of the famous preacher, John Jones of Talasrn, and he combined much of the old fervour with a rare serenity of spirit in the midst of intellectual turmoil. He revealed an acquaintance with the works of Bacon, Copernicus, Brahe, Kepler, Galileo, Newton, Herschel, Franklin, Huyghens, Lamarck, Darwin and Wallace. He was aware of the disturbing nature of many recent hypotheses, including that of Evolution; many of these novelties were, in his view, not free from difficulties but the theory of Evolution was "accepted by a large number of the leading naturalists of our age". He was therefore in no position to dismiss the theory but he issued a warning against applying a similar hypothesis to explain social and religious phenomena; this had happened in the work of Baur, Keim, Strauss and Renan who had eradicated all supernatural elements from the life of Christ Himself. Jones asserted his conviction that the evidence for the pivotal supernatural event of Christ's resurrection was overwhelming and could only be rejected by an unbelieving spirit (1904, 21-9).

A similar confidence was displayed by Rev. T. G. Owen, M.A., Liverpool, in his valedictory address in 1912. He spoke of the great changes brought about by the development of electricity and wireless telegraphy. There was a fore-shadowing of nuclear fission in his quotation of a recent speech at the British Association which referred to an impending revelation in the world of matter. Travel was also being revolutionised; journeys which once took four or five days could now be made in as many hours, and a transatlantic journey had been cut from four or five weeks to as many days. With the advent of aeroplanes it was possible to make "a flight across the Channel in safety even with a passenger on board". Pensions for the old and a living wage for workers were within sight of being realised (1912, 23-7).

It would have been surprising if there had been no voices raised in alarm at all the material advances and at the winds of changing thought. In 1900 Rev. C. T. Astley, M.A., Llandudno, launched a spirited attack upon Darwin and his theory of Evolution which he said was "the most senseless and scienceless idea that ever entered the brain of a great man"; he claimed that he had given Darwin's thesis thirty years to live and that the passage of time was proving the theory to be nothing more than a passing dream (1900, 33).

While theories about the Creation caused turmoil even greater unrest was caused by the novel developments in the study of the Bible. In a Conference sermon in 1894 Rev. William Williams, Swansea, said that recent attacks upon the books of Moses were heretical. He claimed that Colenso's work was as dead as a nail before he died. The recent study of Colenso by Prof. Hinchcliff comes to a not dissimilar conclusion, but if the excesses of Colenso's work have withered away the critical method was not discredited and the situation could not return to what it had been before Colenso's work was published. Williams then made the telling point which has been emphasised in all recent criticism of Liberalism in theology that the methods of criticism were based on the assumption that progress was always by evolution rather than by revelation. However, his application of this point was less than convincing. He summarised the critical position fairly enough by stating that it held the books of Moses reflected a stage of thought and life which could not have been actual in the time of Moses and therefore these books were written, or at least edited, in the age of Josiah or even of the Maccabees. Williams held that such theories were refuted by Christ's own testimony to Mosaic authorship. Williams also allowed that many of the critics were good and devout men but their goodness was the residue of their convictions before they began to feed on fare provided by "German cooks", and for himself he held that it would be more honourable to fight under the flag of the old views and if necessary to die wrapped up therein than be seen under a banner with a strange device which had been manufactured in Germany and then patched up in England to make it look respectable (1894, 19-20).

The new trends of study could not be stemmed by mere flights of oratory and there were others who believed that while the new ranges of knowledge could not be ignored the central message of the Gospel had not been weakened. The faith was unchanging though wrapped in an ever-changing vesture. For example, Principal Prys spoke calmly and constructively in 1903 about the ferment in the Church. He said that the comparatively recent emancipation of human thought was bound to lead to some turbulence which could not be forcibly quelled; "Exercise no compulsion, else this heavenly guest will never enter the door". He thought that the initial fury of attacks by theoretical materialism, atheistic naturalism, agnosticism, and pantheism had abated though many of these views were still peddled in the products of the Rationalist Press. He cited Haeckel's *Riddle of the Universe* where it was assumed that the Christian case for the genuineness of the four Gospels rested on the tale that these four had miraculously leaped on the table at the Council of Nicea and had separated themselves from a mass of contradictory and forged manuscripts. No intelligent Christian held such a view. He also admitted that recent studies would lead to modifications of prevailing views "on the truths of Scripture as well as the truth concerning Scripture", but this process of correction was not new and need not be feared (1903, 19-22).

By 1910 the dust of battle had somewhat settled and Rev. E. O. Davies, B.SC.,[8] Llandudno, could say that he knew no one who now held the dictation theory of Scripture. The human element was too obvious to allow for any such theory. It did not follow that the Bible would therefore pass away as a transient phenomenon in the course of the evolution of religion. Jesus Christ was too central to allow for such a theory. Even though a kenosis of some kind had to be granted there was no evading "the infallible authority of the Son of God in relation to matters of belief and conduct". Davies even allowed that the Gospels had undergone editorial shaping in the process of transmission so that in their present form they did not come direct from the first circle of disciples but they were nevertheless authorities of the first order, and the interpretation of Christ therein came from the Apostles who had exceptional advantages and whose witness must be normative for all time (1910, 26-32). Rev. Richard Hughes, M.A., Aberystwyth, also referred to the many "well-assured results of critical investigation" whose outcome was not to weaken faith but to enable the reader to discern the things which could not be shaken and to gain fresh guidance for the strengthening of character and the purifying of conduct. God revealed Himself in changing vestures, and in history God had been "weaving the garments through which He sought to make Himself visible to His children". God had made Himself to be seen in Scripture, experience, and Jesus Christ, and through these intimations He "is training us for the beatific vision" (1910, 35-41). Rev. R. R. Roberts returned to this theme in his valedictory presidential address in 1913 and said that the new studies had given Christ a new pre-eminence. The Bible had lost that equality of value in all its parts which sometimes proved to be a hindrance to the vision of Christ. "We shall judge everything in relation to Him, and we shall count nothing authoritative that is not sanctioned by His Spirit" ; "an absolute faith in Christ will fear no new light" (1913, 17). Rev. J. Morgan Jones, M.A., Merthyr, stated plainly in 1925 that he accepted the documentary hypothesis of the composition of the early chapters of Genesis and he found this to be a valuable aid to understanding the Bible. Many strands and sources had come together in the Bible, and he dated Genesis about 500 B.C. He regretted, as many have done since, the indiscriminate use of such terms as myth, saga and legend, because though there were elements in Genesis which could be traced back to such sources the end product was neither myth nor saga nor legend. Neither was Genesis a scientific document; this meant that many misconceptions and common beliefs had to be surrendered, but the Word of God shone through the words as never before. Rev. W. J. Clothier, B.D., Swansea, also emphasised the importance of realising the basic aim of the Bible which he defined as the record of God's work in the lives of men, a manual of devotion, and a story culminating in the revelation in Jesus Christ (1925, 22-7). Rev. C. Vincent Williams, Llanelli, also saw great gain in recent studies; many statements in the Old Testament attributed thoughts and commands to God which were hard to reconcile with the New Testament revelation; Calvin could hold that the Old Testament statements reflected the way God Himself made men to think about Him, but now they could be taken to indicate how men thought of God at that time (1927, 26-9).

Oratory can, however, camouflage many shades of meaning so that speakers often think they are in agreement when they are in fact using the same words but with different meanings. Rev. D. M. Rees in his retiring presidential address in 1928 said that "the Scriptures remain unbroken, infallible, eternal, the standard of faith, the rule of life, the impregnable rock of God"; this seemed strong enough but he also said that criticism had cleared off moss and earth and debris so that the unchanging granite might gleam ever brighter. The verbal garments might change but the truth was unchanging. Rees' understanding of infallibility was therefore quite different from that of others who would have denied the presence of moss or earth or debris in the Scriptures, and he was almost at one with others who said they were rejecting the idea of infallibility. He wound up with the practical advice to preachers that their message, if faithful to the Gospel, ought to be one of optimism and not pessimism, positive and constructive, and not negative and critical; it ought to nourish faith, not doubt (1928, 25-6).

Prof. G. A. Edwards, Bala, set forth his view of the Bible in 1929. God's character did not change but men grew in their ability to receive and understand fuller revelation. The Biblical writers were not machines or amanuenses and their writings were not free from inconsistencies. Nor was Edwards satisfied with the theory that though God did not dictate the Bible he so overruled man's efforts as to produce an infallible book. Edwards preferred to think of the prophetic insight which lay behind the Bible; the prophet's mind and conscience both worked freely as they saw and experienced the truth which eventually was embodied in the words of the Bible (1929, 27-31).

The complexity of the theme of infallibility was further illustrated in 1929 by Rev. Ieuan Phillips, B.A., who in 1966 was the Moderator of the General Assembly; he affirmed his belief in the infallibility of the Bible and was convinced that the Bible claimed this for itself (1929, 37). The decades since 1929 have shown that terms such as infallibility have such a wide connotation that definition is essential to any understanding thereof.

These controversial issues arising from contemporary movements of thought inevitably led to questions as to the Church's confessional position. Accepted dogmas came under fire but the Church had bound itself in the past to a dogmatic position. Some held that the only honest policy for deviationists was to resign from any office they held in the Connexion; some were even ready to hunt and hound out heretics. In 1894 Rev. William Williams, Swansea, said that many people regarded laxity as evidence of superior intellectuality and were ready to surrender truth for the sake of a quiet life; though it was common to regard heresy-hunting as a very disreputable occupation he felt it necessary to issue a warning against heresies (1894, 17-8). However, the prevailing trend of thought was that the Connexion would be better served by a reasonable defence of its teaching than by a forced submission to authority. This was expressed with characteristic brilliance by Prof. Ellis Edwards. He said that the Connexion had been built upon a definite system of beliefs which were now under assault. The attacks needed to be faced and examined; where necessary, they had to be refuted, but where they were justified the Church had to profit thereby and revise its position. There was no ground for a spineless abdication of the intellectual cogency of the Christian position and Edwards went on to set forth a statement of what he conceived to be the main Christian truths :

We believe in the divine place of Jesus Christ, and the unique importance of His teachings, His work, His aid.

We believe that there is direct approach to Him for every soul.

We believe that His grace may produce in every heart a lasting miracle, giving it a superhuman power which is yet the only power that can make it fully human.

We believe faith alone is sufficient to unite all men to Himself.

We believe the Spirit of Christ is an exhaustless force, able to raise the worst of men to heights not yet conceived by any.

We believe that preaching and the other parts of the Church's work are means by which this power may be offered, obtained and constantly increased, that no other means for their special purposes are as effectual, and that to be slack or neglectful in their use is to diminish or withhold from men the possibilities of the greatest blessing, to be unfaithful to love, to be wanting in simple humanity, to pass by sin, weakness, misery, without offering the most effectual help (1900, 24).

Thus at the turn of the century the Conference had in Prof. Edwards a President who held that the Church had a message to proclaim and was not afraid to submit it to intellectual scrutiny. In 1903 Principal Owen Prys also stated that truth was not bound up with immutable statements of Christian doctrines (1903, 19-22). In 1908 the President, Rev. J. Glyn Davies, issued a warning against heresy-hunters who would light again the fires of Smithfield in Wales if they could; he claimed that the Connexion's Confession of Faith was the best ever published but even it was not final; he himself had no desire for any new theology but he wanted fair play for fresh views and held that the proper way to meet error was not to persecute it but to expose it for the error it was (1908, 86-7). Mr. John Owens, J.P., Chester, said the Church was not slavishly bound to inherited interpretations but could modify them as required in the light of scholarship and experience (1908, 88).

In 1913 Rev. R. R. Roberts, in his retiring address as President, said the Church was not simply on a voyage of discovery nor did it exist for the sake of speculation. It had a message to proclaim. Christ was risen and the Church had to reflect His Light. Yet he was not apprehensive about variety of opinion nor would he seek to stifle it because truth was its own defence; moreover, schism and heresy, painful as they were, often led to a deeper grasp of the truth (1913, 16-7). In 1920 Rev. Evan Armstrong, Ebbw Vale, admitted the difficulty in being a Church with standards and at the same time allowing for liberty of thought. Zeal for dogmatic positions often led to bigotry which became so over-riding that "a man who views a sceptic with complacency is stirred up to bitter wrath by the sight of a fellow Christian who does not utter his sectarian shibboleth", and Christian love was then reserved to those sharing the same ecclesiastical outlook and "such a love is simply enlarged selfishness". Moreover "those who make extraordinary pretensions to holiness" were often the most obvious transgressors of the law of love. "Censoriousness is a deadly sin". Christians were called to the difficult task of "conciliation without compromise" and this required great patience, for good people could often be cantankerous and religion often seemed to stir up all that was disagreeable in men (1920, 30).

In 1919 a Reconstruction Commission was set up by the two Associations and it reported its "unhesitating belief in the right of the Church to revise its creed whenever it feels that such a revision is necessary". However, as early as 1892 Rev. D. C. Edwards said that whatever the formal position of the Connexion as a body individual ministers were already at liberty since, unlike other Presbyterian Churches, they were not required to sign and subscribe to Articles of Faith. He held that this was a wise policy since, also unlike other Presbyterian Churches, there had been no trouble over heresies for more than fifty years (1892, 15). However it is possible to hold that the assent made at inductions to "preach the Gospel of Jesus in its richness and fulness" meant more than a promise to preach what each minister regarded as the Gospel.

After 1900 many speakers, especially from among the laity showed a keen interest in changes in the theological climate. Mr. J. R. Davies, J.P., in his retiring address as President in 1902 said that many questions of theology, creed and organisation were but the spray and surf on the waves of the great ocean of Life and were not of central importance for the religious life. Churches tended to invest their traditions with the unchangeability which belonged to divinity and to assume that "the Creeds and methods of a century gone by are those of the Church to-day". In his view, while the Church had been waiting for history to repeat itself the Spirit of God had moved on the masses outside the Church. The Cross of Christ had leavened the world more than the Church suspected and had taken a large place in the hearts of men outside the churches. There was therefore need for the Church to recognise this and to make room for larger liberty in the expression of truth and to allow a larger welcome to the Lord's Table. He disagreed with the current policy as a result of which the great majority of those connected with the Connexion were not communicants but only adherents who felt the invitation to the Lord's Table was not for them (1902, 17-8). Rev. J. H. Owen, Pembroke, took up this point and admitted that all there was of Christianity was not to be found in the churches. There was a wider leaven in the world. In contrast to those who held that indifference increased where the Church failed to instil a knowledge of its doctrines Owen held that many were repelled by the insistence upon dogma. In his view, many who were clever in doctrinal disputation, quick in detecting schism or adept in discerning ceremonial variations, were often quite indifferent to the central truth of the Gospel (1902, 29-30). Mr. John Owens, J.P., said in 1923 that there was less danger from efforts to restate doctrine than from clinging to antiquated forms and that while people did not want an undogmatic religion they did want dogmas taught frankly and also progressing through change. (1923, 10).

Principal Prys spoke in 1926 on the necessity for theology. Theology was an attempt to express the nature of the reality revealed in religious experience. It was a derivative product but every religious experience had to be followed up by some degree of theologising so as to lift the experience from excessive subjectivity (1926, 21-5). This theme was followed up in characteristic style by Rev. R. M. Roberts, B.A., B.D., then a young minister and destined to be one of the architects of the Association in the East and a statesman of the whole Connexion. He said theology was necessary as a means of communication and of clarification but it ought not to be allowed to become the static definition of fixed positions. Theology was rather the quest for truth, and it required disinterestedness, humility and an adventurous progress (1926, 27-31).

In the years after the First War there was a tendency to minimise the importance of theology but by 1927 there were signs that Karl Barth's influence in the renewal of theology was being felt in Wales. The reaction was generally unfavourable at first. Rev. C. Vincent Williams, M.A., Llanelly, questioned Barth's methods of expounding the transcendence of God : "He has published a study on the *Epistle to the Romans* in which he refuses to pay any attention to the usual topics of historical, literary and textual criticism, and he has the annoying habit of assuming that his views are the views of St. Paul". Certainly Paul did defend the arbitrary action on the part of God and it must appear even more arbitrary if God was so wholly other as Barth described him to be. However, though Paul did not pursue his premises with the ruthless logic of Calvin there was little point in trying to show that Paul did not teach a doctrine of Election or in trying to dissolve it into an election to service. In 1929 Rev. Philip J. Jones, M.A., B.D., Cardiff, assailed Barth's teaching as the work of a panic-stricken apocalypticist. He said that the Barthian school claimed to emancipate theology from the psychological subjectivism which had reigned since Schleiermacher but Williams found Barth's work to be extremely superficial despite its formidable style and aggressive manner (1923, 32-3). Jones' understanding of Barth was challenged by Rev. Aethwy Jones, M.A., Liverpool, who said that Jones had missed Barth's main contention which was that after all has been said about the history, morality and revelation in the Bible there could still be a failure to touch the real Word of God in the Bible (1929, 37).

In all the Conferences there was a constant reference to the centrality of Christ for the understanding of God and his ways, but theology was far from being a static study reiterating the dogmas of bygone ages. There was an awareness of the tradition of Scripture interpretation in the Church and there was also openness to the winds of change which were blowing at the turn of the century and in the years before and after the Great War. The Conferences made clear that Welsh Presbyterianism, in common with most branches of the Church, passed through a period when the value of theology was minimized. There was need of some softening of the earlier aridities but the change was not all gain; the resulting theological confusion was probably one of the causes of the later weakness of the denominations. There were voices echoing the challenge of Barth and recalling the Church to a serious study of theology, but though he had considerable influence in Wales he never became a dominant figure in Welsh theological study.

Chapter IV

CHURCH RELATIONS

No survey of the Conferences can fail to note that the Connexion was keenly aware of the existence of other denominations in Wales. The Connexion had originally started as a movement of reform within the Established Church and there was particularly keen interest in the condition of that Church. There was strong support for the disestablishment of that Church from its privileged position and it is of interest to compare the fiery phillipics heard in the early Conferences with the milder tone of speeches made after Disestablishment took place in 1920. Memories of old hostilities and of indignities suffered at the hands of Anglican squires and clergy rankled in the Connexional mind, and there was keen resentment of continuing disabilities. The alleged increase of sacerdotalism within Anglicanism and the position of the children of nonconformist parents in schools controlled by the Church of England were topics frequently discussed.

Rev. D. Charles Edwards, Merthyr, a son of Lewis Edwards, repudiated Anglican claims "to have received a peculiar virtue along the tips of lawn-sleeved bishops through the darkness of the Middle Ages" (1892, 7); he also looked back to the libertine gentry and semi-sceptical bishops whose conduct had forced the Calvinistic Methodists to secede from the Church of England (1894, 65-6). In 1893 Rev. Thomas Rees, Merthyr, assailed the ritualism of "disguised Popery" which was invading the Principality; he did not deny that there were well-meaning Christians connected with the Oxford Movement but he regarded the growth of these "grotesque" mummeries as a baneful influence which reduced salvation to a routine of bodily exercises. It was easier, according to Rees, to be "a pompous celebrant than a powerful effective preacher" (1893, 34). In 1894 an address of welcome to the Conference from the Chester Free Church Council said that sacerdotalism was a great peril to the Church and added to the unbelief and practical ungodliness which were so prevalent (1894, 21). Dr. Ebenezer Davies, Medical Officer of Health for Swansea, referred to the same topic in his retiring address as President. He said there was a longing in the Evangelical sections of the Church of England for reunion and he himself was not unduly perturbed by the prospect of government by "the historic episcopate". The Methodist Episcopal example in America was encouraging. Nevertheless he feared the absorption of their Church by those whose "sacerdotal claims" for the clergy challenged the completeness of Christ's atonement. As long as this doctrine was taught "overtures for reunion will lack weight and authority" (1894, 31). In 1895 Mr. Owen Owen, M.A., J.P., Master of the High School in Oswestry, said that sacredotalism in the Church "is as serious a social danger as collectivism in the state, for here we have religion made easy with no special need for spiritual effort" (1895, 37). Rev. Williams James, Manchester, made a fiery speech on the same topic. In his view, a claim to apostolic succession was a "monstrous absurdity and a huge imposture,—a glaring mockery, a shameful hypocrisy"; he regarded the vestments associated with the priesthood in its Roman, Orthodox, and Anglican manifestations as "grotesque tailoring" and a "load of priestly paraphernalia". As for a succession of bishops from the Apostles "the absurdity of such a postulate is plain to every unsophisticated mind"; there was no evidence to prove "a priestly pedigree one half the length of the labyrinthine chain"; some of the links were rusty, besmired, and rotten. James held there was urgent need for a campaign against "the tyranny of a self-constituted and self-seeking priestcraft which was inimical to the best interests of humanity, antagonistic to the liberty of the person, intellect or conscience, and blighting to all free development of true manliness". He castigated all sacerdotal performances and their attendant accessories whether forged in the moulds of prelatic Canterbury or smelted in the furances of pontifical Rome (1895, 48-53). Rev. Richard Hughes, Aberystwyth, covered similar ground though with less pyrotechnical zest and he held that the persistence of sacerdotal ideas was due to the fact that they were a perversion of the truth that there was a priesthood of the whole Church which had been given the promise of supernatural guidance (1895, 53-4). In 1896 Rev. T. J. Wheldon, B.A., said that "sacerdotalism is rampant among us" (1896, 50). Rev. Evan Williams, Abermule, spoke of the "sacerdotalism which is surging around us" (1896, 61). Alderman Jones Griffiths spoke of "the mildew upon the dry rot of superstition" (1896, 78).

In 1904 Rev. J. M. Saunders, M.A., referred to sacerdotal utterances by Anglican clergy which "are enough to appal any man who has an open Bible before him" and which issued from many clergy and not just from a "handful of effeminate curates". In the past one would have had to go ten miles to see a High Churchman but now one would have to go ten miles to see a Low Churchman (1904, 54). This verdict, however, ill accords with the scathing verdict passed by Methodist preachers upon earlier generations of clergy.

Saunders, however, held that the spread of sacerdotal ideas was not the main reason for opposing the Established Church. The main rock of offence was the very fact of establishment. This had already been raised by the retiring President, Mr. William Evans, J.P., Southport, in 1898 when he looked forward to the snapping "once and for ever the fetters which now bind the Church of England hand and foot to the State", and then her arrogance would cease and the traitors who yearned for papal recognition would be swept away (1895, 25). Saunders held that establishment denied "what we call the voluntary principle in religion" and introduced elements of coercion and discrimination which violated the very essence of the Gospel. Even though disestablishment might allow sacerdotal ideas to spread even more widely that was a risk that had to be taken (1904, 55). Rev. A. Wynne Thomas, Aberystwyth, praised the American system where all people were treated as people and were not under "the tyranny of an Established Church" (1904, 52). Rev. James Travis, Chester, branded the Church of England as a political institution whose bishops voted in the House of Lords on the side of privilege and monopoly and against democracy, and whose doctrines were determined by politicians (1904, 59).

Establishment was resented because it gave the Anglican Church a privileged position with consequent irritating disabilities for non-conformists. In 1896 Rev. J. R. Hughes spoke eloquently about the hardships endured in matters of marriage and burial. He alleged that such liberty as the non-conformists had was a mere toleration forced upon the Establishment by political expedience but it was far from liberty or equality. "Why should we as Free Church ministers be shadowed constantly by a state detective in the shape of a registrar when we go to perform the sacred rite of marriage at our respective places of worship?" He said it was an intolerable grievance when it was held that a marriage could be more efficiently performed by the Bishop of St. Asaph or the Dean of Bangor than by Free Church ministers. Moreover, burial fees had to be given to the parson when Free Church ministers "bury our dead in any portion of God's acre", and it was painful to think of the minister standing bare-headed in the rain while the parson sat in his cosy parlour in his easy chair "enjoying his pipe, his claret and his joke at our expense" (1896, 46).

Non-conformists had also often had great difficulty in securing ground for their chapels. Rev. Wynn Davies, Liverpool, told of a peer who refused a site because in his view the Calvinistic Methodists preached politics and not the Gospel. Davies said that his threat to send his lordship a bundle of his sermons had been sufficient to make the peer not only change his mind and grant a site but he also sent a cheque for £25 and exonerated the ministers from his heinous charges. Davies thought that the peer's early obstruction had been due to "the tyrannical influence of another religious sect" (1902, 68).

The virtual Anglican monopoly of the control of education, particularly in the rural areas, was the most exacerbating source of friction. In 1902 a resolution was passed condemning a proposed Bill which, in the view of the Conference, would perpetuate clerical control in 7470 parishes in England and Wales where the Church of England school was the only school and wherein the principles of the Established Church were instilled into the pupils. Moreover, 1177 Church of England schools would be wholly maintained from the public purse but no nonconformist teachers would be employed therein and thus there would be a violation of the constitutional principle that there ought to be public oversight of the use of public money. Further, the Conference held that such a Bill had not been among the issues at the previous election and therefore the government would be using its majority to pass a Bill for which they had no mandate from the people. The Conference therefore called upon the government to withdraw the Bill and threatened to use every available means to obstruct its application even if passed (1902, 10). This declaration was followed up by a speech by Rev. Arthur Wynne Thomas, Aberystwyth, who said that loyalty to Christ often meant insistence on what many would regard as trifles, such as a refusal to pay the education rate even though it was only a matter of a few shillings. The government which was in power largely by the support of non-conformists was now going to use its power to betray the non-conformists by putting elementary education under "an exclusive and arrogant and intolerant Church", and thus in fact endowing afresh the Anglican Church (1902, 44). Not all were in favour of practical obstruction of the government's plans. The retiring President, Mr. J.

R. Davies, J.P., deplored the suggestion of a cheap martyrdom by refusing to pay rates and thus trying to frighten the government; he said such conduct was not worthy of a free, self-respecting and sober-minded people and displayed a lack of faith in themselves, in mankind and in God (1902, 18). Nevertheless, the general tone of the Conferences at this time was one of outraged feelings; it was believed that a grave injustice was being inflicted upon the non-conformists. In 1903 the Conference protested against the violation of the principles of religious liberty and stated that the only way open to non-conformists was the passive resistance of refusal to pay rates (1903, 12). Rev. James Baillie, Cardiff devoted his conference sermon in 1903 to the threat to non-conformity involved in the Education Act. He said that the non-conformists were the great spiritual and political power in the Principality, but the Church of England was trying to undermine that pre-eminence by proselytizing non-conformist children who often had no choice but to attend schools under clerical control. However, in his view, non-conformists were prepared for eviction and imprisonment rather than submit to such insiduous influences being exercised upon their children. Baillie observed that a recent census carried out by the *Daily News* had claimed that people were becoming deaf to the voice of the preacher but with what must now appear considerable brashness he claimed that the proper reading of the data was that people were tired of "ritual, of incense, and of priests". He claimed that while non-conformists were holding their own the Church of England had lost 140,000 members in sixteen years, presumably in Britain (1903, 15-7). In 1904 a resolution was passed in similar terms to that of 1903 but it was noted that County Councils had tried to ease the impact of the Bill upon non-conformists though the threat of coercion still hung over them; the Conference claimed that the aim must be the repeal of the Act. Rev. Henry Rees said that if nonconformists united they could "cast the Education Act into the bottomless pit from whence it came" (1904, 10-5). Rev. J. M. Saunders said that the Education Act was a bold and impudent attempt to crush non-conformists out of existence. He said the new boldness and "jingoism" on the part of the Anglicans arose from an increase in their number during the preceding quarter of a century but, in his view the manoeuvre had failed though it had involved the non-conformists in much suffering (1904, 56). His admission of an increase in Anglican numbers was a contrast to Baillie's assertion of Anglican decline.

Rev. James Travis, Chester, did not seem so confident that victory had been won ; the Act had the effect of excluding non-conformists from head-teacherships, even from assistantships in more than half of the schools of the country which were maintained at public cost (1904, 59).

The winds of discord abated considerably after 1920 ; the War broke down many barriers and all Churches felt themselves to be up against a spirit corrosive of all religion. In 1929 the retiring President, Rev. J. H. Davies, Ewloe Green, spoke of the need of religious instruction in schools. He felt there was more common ground among the Churches and the opposition to Bible teaching in schools was less stubborn than it had been twenty years ago. The Churches had had friendly talks, and teachers and education authorities were combining to provide schemes of Religious Instruction. He hoped that such courses could be coordinated with the Sunday School lessons (1929, 23-4). Rev. John Edwards said in his retiring presidential address in 1931 that while there had been need to protest against state subsidies for the teaching of sectarian creeds there had been great losses due to the sectarian strife ; among these he counted the omission from the 1870 Education Act of any provision for Bible-teaching ; this had been "one of our forefathers' greatest blunders" (1931, 21).

It is however specially significant to note the tributes paid to Anglicanism even in the midst of sectarian strife. As early as 1894 Dr. Cynddylan Jones spoke in unusually cordial terms when the Conference was welcomed to Chester by Alderman Charles Brown, J.P., the Deputy-Mayor and an Anglican. Dr. Jones admitted that relations between Churchmen and non-conformists were "a little bit estranged" but he had no doubt the day would come when they would stand shoulder to shoulder on behalf of religion and of raising the masses to a higher level of morality (1894, 51-52). In 1894 Rev. D. C. Edwards, though attacking what he regarded as the corruptions of the Church of England, said that the Calvinistic Methodist Fathers had not differed from the doctrines taught in the Church of England nor had they had any conscientious scruples about episcopal ordination (1894, 65). In 1896 it was reported that many representatives attending the Oswestry Conference had been accommodated in homes of members of the Church of England, and Rev. D. D. Williams hoped that Presbyterians would reciprocate and offer hospitality to delegates who would be attending the forthcoming Anglican Congress to be held in Shrewsbury (1896, 88).

A most remarkable tribute to the Church of England was paid in 1903 by Principal Owen Prys. He said that in spite of a sacerdotal section in that Church it was as a whole faithful to the Evangelical Faith and no one ought to forget that it was a "branch of Christ's Church". He said that while involved in controversy with the Church of England, "I hope I shall never forget to treat it as one Christian ought to treat another. We owe too much to the saints and thinkers of that Church not to deplore the present controversy and the occasion of it". This controversy was "a cause of real pain to all who are truly concerned for the interest of Christ's Church", and Prys hoped that the breach between them would soon be healed, although it must be at the cost of Disestablishment (1903, 27). In 1908 the President, Rev. J. Glyn Davies, said of the Church of England that he admired "the culture and consecration of its ministry, the grace and glory of its ritual, and the variety and amplitude of its resources" ; he said, "It is a great Christian Church", and referring especially to its liturgy he said he admired the chasteness of its diction, the charm of its phrasing, the fitness of its prayers, and the reverence of its tone (1908, 85-6). In 1911 the President, Alderman S. N. Jones regretted that no Anglican representatives were present ; he rejoiced that the Bishop of Llandaff had recently addressed the Wesleyan Conference at Cardiff and he was sure that Presbyterians would have welcomed Bishop Owen of St. Davids whose "blood is blue Calvinistic Methodist blood" (1911, 11). The first Anglican representative to be received officially by the Conference was the Bishop of Chester. Bishop Mercer addressed the Conference when it visited Chester in 1919 and it was probably easier for him than it would have been for a Welsh bishop to welcome a Conference on Welsh soil. English bishops were naturally less hampered by bitter memories. Bishop Mercer said that wild forces had been let loose in the world during the War and in the consequent industrial unrest. Unless the Churches had something to say in such circumstances it was doubtful if their continued existence was justified. He doubted if divided Churches could say the necessary word. Continued division meant that thousands of children in state schools got no religious education. Bishop Mercer also had the attitude typical of many bishops of the period that he was not enamoured with ritual but was eager to retain the establishment. However, he had a vision of a comprehensive Church which could prove to the world its love for the one Saviour (1919, 16). Puleston Jones welcomed the bishop's remarks and said he had now changed his mind from the view that religion should be kept out of day schools. Teachers could now have made the system work but it was the politicians who were now hesitant. He held that union need not wait upon full agreement on every issue. For example, he himself would not quarrel within a united Church with those who wanted more ritual than he did. There was need for more than mere toleration of one another, indeed for more than federation ; there was need for real understanding and comprehension of one another (1919, 17-8).

The ice having been broken by Bishop Mercer, the succeeding conferences were addressed by a succession of Welsh clergy of varying degrees of ecclesiastical dignity though no Welsh bishop attended before the series of conferences ended in 1938. Rev. D. E. Llewellyn Jones, Vicar of Maindee, said in 1920 that Christ had prayed in the first century for the spirit of unity and this was still necessary in the twentieth if the Church was to face the problems of the time (1920, 3). In 1921 the Dean of Bangor, Very Rev. Griffith Roberts, told the Conference that contrary to his own expectations the coming of Disestablishment had been followed by a greater brotherliness between Churchmen and non-conformists than he had ever known (1921, 3). In 1922 Prebendary Wilson, the Vicar of Swansea, said he looked forward to the early accomplishment of "one Church of Christ to which we are all sending our particular contribution" (1922, 8).

Fraternal greetings without any commitment however give little clue to the reality of obstacles and in 1923 Mr. J. Mortimer Harris of Hoylake introduced a salutary realism into the growing euphoria and said that he did not think that denominationalism was a hindrance to unity but could co-exist with a genuine respect for each others' convictions. He saw the presence of the Anglican clergy as no sign that they wished to become Presbyterians and he himself had no wish to become an Anglican. Canon C. Brooke-Gwynne, West Kirkby, replied and said that religious differences were the price of liberty and he did not think the price was too great (1923, 3-4). In 1932 the Rector of Neath said that as Churches came together they were lifted out of their parochialism and they could co-operate against what he called the gadfly of secularism ; he did not see why this could not occur while still divided by matters of doctrine and order (1932, 9).

When the Conference met in Pontypridd in 1928 a welcome was extended by the local League of Churches which included all with the exception of the Roman Catholic Church. This must have been one of the earliest Councils in the Country (1928, 9).

Relations with other non-conformist groups were harmonious, at least on paper. The movement for the establishment of Free Church Councils had been in full swing and wherever the conferences met delegates from the local Free Church Councils extended a welcome. Their theme was invariably the value of co-operation against rampant evils but there were few indications of any awareness for the need of corporate unity. Indeed, there was considerable support for the view that denominational rivalry was a valuable asset. In 1896 Rev. David Rees, a Welsh Baptist delegate, told the Conference that a healthy competition among Christians was not a hindrance but a great help to the progress of the Church of Christ (1896, 26). In 1897 another Baptist, Rev. James Owen, told the Swansea Conference that no union based on compromise could be worth anything ; a lasting union could not be brought about by ecclesiastical soldering but by God (1897, 20). In fairness to Presbyterians it has to be admitted that constitutionally Baptists and Independants were more tied to ideas of separatism than were Presbyterians.

The tone of Presbyterian speeches was usually more constructive and conciliatory. As always, Dr. Cynddylan Jones spoke with realistic freshness and surveyed relations with other denominations. He was pleased to note that after decades of tension with the Wesleyans the two bodies were drawing together and he saw great value in wedding the practical stress of the Wesleyans to the solid attachment of Calvinistic Methodists to high doctrines of the mysterious working of God. A practical concern did not involve a recession from the high and deep things of God. He paid tribute also to the work of the seventeenth century Independent Pioneer, Dr. John Owen, "your noblest representative". He classed Owen's work, *The Person and Glory of Christ,* among the hundred best books and he was so close to its teaching that if the Independents could adopt Presbyterian Church government the wall of partition could fall within a year. Referring to the Baptists, he paid tribute to their struggle for civil and religious liberty, but he admitted the reality of the river dividing them, and though he could not accept the Baptist invitation to meet them in the middle of the river he was ready to salute them from the bank in the Master's name (1894, 24-5). In the same year, Dr. Ebenezer Davies, Swansea, while surveying relations with other Churches, particularly with the Anglicans, set forth a noble vision. There was, in his view, an existing unity which did not wait for uniformity. The guarantee of a brighter future lay in Christ's prayer that His people might be one. Dr. Davies then gave a graphic illustration of his point; when the tide was out there were numerous little pools on the shore, each with its complement of fishes and each cut off from the other, but when the tide pouted in then the pools merged together and their tenants met; so, Churches were divided by the ebb-tides of history but when the Spirit poured in then the denominational pools would be merged by glad waters "in whose ample depths the saints on earth have room to range"; "happy Church whose sectarianism shall first be swept away in this inundation of love and joy" (1894, 31-2). Dr. Davies, like most laymen, had little relish for sectarian strife. Mr. Edward Jones of Thackery St. Church referred to "the undue and ruinous competitions" in the villages and rural areas of Wales.

In 1903 Principal Owen Prys said it was sad to see three or four weak and inefficient churches all claiming to be evangelical where one would suffice and be efficient (1903, 25). He hoped that the Free Churches would come closer. There had been serious causes of separation in the past and the different denominations represented different aspects of religious truth but jealousy between denominations was evil and he looked forward to the day when there would be a Free Evangelical Church of Wales (1903, 9). The time for this was not yet ripe but Churches were learning from each other and the Faith which united them was greater than opinions which divided them. Moreover, the approaching struggle with rationalism would show that their differences were insignificant (1903, 25-7). In 1912 the President, Rev. T. G. Owen, said "it is time we, the Free Churches, united our forces and closed our ranks" (1912, 10). In 1913 Rev. R. R. Roberts, in his retiring presidential address, said that inter-denominational controversy arose because of their distance from Christ who is the common denominator of all the Creeds and until there was a mystical union with the transcendent Christ any formal unity brought into being as a result of a round-table conference with mutual concessions of convictions would not be a witness to Christ (1913, 20-1). In 1932 the Conference took note of the reunion of Wesleyan Methodism by sending a telegram of greeting to the union meeting then being held in the Albert Hall in London (1932, 10). The President, Rev. R. J. Rees, thought that there was a common spirit leaping over the walls of division and there was a common purpose among the Free Churches (1932, 10). However, not all the aspirations have been able to lead to any effective steps towards realising a unity which all professed to seek. In 1931 Rev. J. J. Morgan, Mold, addressed the ordinands and pled with them to throw their "whole weight and strength into the glorious task of bringing nearer the unity of the universal Church" (1931, 57-63).

Most references to the Roman Catholic Church were hostile in tone though there were appreciative remarks about great figures of the Medieval Church and also to the efficiency and thoroughness of the Roman Church. Sacerdotal ideas were denounced but they were even more bitterly reviled when they appeared among Anglicans who, it was held, should have known better. Rev. D. Charles Edwards could refer to the Pope as "the Man of Sin seated on the seven hills blasphemously calling himself the infallible Vicar of Christ on earth" (1892, 8). Rev. John Hughes, Liverpool, could however see lights in the medieval gloom ; the church of the time was "the Church of God still, the representative of all that the world had inherited from the Apostles" ; there had been evil popes and cardinals but there had also been men like Bernard, Anselm and à Kempis, and in the lives of pious men and women "God had not left His Church in spite of the corruptions of the hierarchy" ; there was in it the continuation of apostolic Christianity (1897, 68). Nevertheless, he denied all special privileges claimed by the hierarchy. "The humblest believer and the proudest cardinal and the most infallible Pope are equidistant from the common centre". He saw in the continuing appeal of the priesthood the paganism of the human heart which responds to gorgeous robes, Gothic architecture, breathing incense, and imaginative fervour (1897, 72). Prof. J. Young Evans, Trevecca, a brilliant classical scholar who had graduated at London and Oxford, and whose hobby was the translation of Latin hymns into Welsh verse and vice versa, attacked the Roman Catholic doctrines and their Anglican counterfeits ; the new Anglicanism was old Romanism. He held that superstition and despotism had been the buttress of the Roman Catholic fabric. He also foreshadowed an increase in "invertebrate tolerance" and envisaged among weak and uninformed minds a yearning for a sensuous ceremonial by which all faith would vanish into a vague feeling of pity and terror and also by which educated people would be driven to the desperation and blasphemy of anarchy and atheism

(1897, 73-74). A medical doctor, Dr. H. Lewis Hughes, deplored the decline in "the hostility to Rome" and said that never before had there been greater ignorance of Protestant principles. He claimed that the Roman Catholic Church had set its sights on Wales as a weak and vulnerable land which would be easily won (1897, 77). In 1898 Mr. William Evans, J.P. spoke in his valedictory address as President about Roman Catholic moves to increase its hold in Wales. It was the hope of recruiting some of the Welsh oratorical gifts into the pre-priesthood which moved Cardinal Vaughan to hold services in Llandrindod Wells where there were practically no Roman Catholics but where staunch Protestants frequently spent a holiday (1898, 25-6). This was also a commentary on the habits of reasonably prosperous farmers and merchants at the turn of the century. In 1904 Rev. James Travis, Chester said he had no fear that "this nation will ever again bend her neck or bow her knee to Rome" (1904, 58). In 1908 a delegate from the Council of English Free Churches in Colwyn Bay told the Conference that the "hydra-headed monster" of Roman Catholicism had recently shown a new aggressiveness and had even "dumped down some of her religious orders in the very heart of the Principality" (1908, 10). Mr. John Owens, Chester, paid tribute to such notable Roman Catholics as à Kempis, Francis, Newman, Manning, and "a host of other good and pious men", but nevertheless he thought the Roman Catholic system to be a perversion of Christianity which was prone to repress and keep people in ignorance and he stressed the need to withstand Roman Catholic attempts to recapture England (1908, 89). However, by 1920 Rev. R. R. Roberts felt able to say that in the face of expanding knowledge "in these days even the Church of Rome is learning a lot of modesty" (1920, 19). However in 1931 the retiring President, Rev. John Edwards, Wrexham, said that it was sad to hear of some Protestants sending their children to Roman Catholic Schools (1931, 21). Mr. J. Mortimer Harris, Chester, noted that it had been said that the Roman Catholic Church was the only Church making headway in Wales ; if this was so, it was not due to the faith or Gospel set forth by that Church but to its highly efficient organisation which was both to be admired and feared (1931, 37).

Rev. E. G. Miles, a minister with Welsh roots who had built up one of the largest and most active churches in the Presbyterian Church of England at Cheam, told the Conference in 1932 that while the Reformation had been a great emancipation it also had painful consequences in a Church still rent from top to bottom with the Roman Catholic Church on one side and the scattered forces of Protestantism on the other ; "this is corporate sin in its blackest form, a Church shrinking back, afraid to go into the fight, to close its ranks and sink its differences" (1932, 49).

Thus, the connexion was stirring with ecumenical winds though there was no clear vision of whither the winds would blow in the future. There was dissatisfaction with the divided Church as it was and yet no clear vision of how the Church could be healed. Even now it would seem that the British Isles and particularly Wales may be the areas in which the answer will be most slow in coming. In 1901 Dr. Griffiths, a missionary of furlough, spoke words which missionaries have often reiterated ; the Church of the future in India would be different from the Church in Britain ; Indian Christians believed it would be one great Church (1901, 75).

The Conferences also sought to keep in touch with the life and thought of other Churches outside Wales, and in particular with Presbyterian Churches, by inviting distinguished preachers to preach during the Conference. The first visitor was Rev. John MacNeill, Regent Square Presbyterian Church, London, and the report of his visit reveals his characteristic humour and quaintness. He preached "a powerful sermon" to a full congregation in Tabernacle, Aberystwyth ; the people listened with "wrapt and admiring attention", and his reading of the Scripture was "interspersed with running comments which were much enjoyed". He also took part in the Conference discussions at the invitation of the President, Dr. T. C. Edwards, and he rebuked members for their timidity in discussion and for their unprofitable questions (1889, 17-8).

In 1894 Prof. George Adam Smith preached what one listener called "a heart-refreshing sermon" on Psalm 23 (1894, 46). There were many other visitors, such as Prof. James Denney, whose sermons were in the same solid expository tradition.

Rev. Dr. J. Guiness Rogers visited the Conference in 1897 ; he was a distinguished and uncompromising Independent strongly opposed to Establishment ; "I want to root out State Churches wherever they exist". He was not against any Church choosing its own form of government, episcopal or otherwise, but he wished to end state interference with any Church and he regretted the failure of a recent

Bill to disestablish the Church of England to reach the Statute Book. He held that the Free Churches were in great danger of losing their hard-won liberties through Anglican devices such as reunion conferences, diplomatic circulars, and kindly messages. It is doubtful if even his Welsh hearers with all their fears of Anglicanism would have entirely subscribed to such a sinister interpretation of every Anglican move ; Presbyterians had a sense of Connexional solidarity that rendered Independent isolation almost as unpalatable as centralised Anglicanism or Romanism.

Rogers, who could be negative on this issue, then took to task those whose policy was little more than a negative attitude to beer, tobacco, the theatre, and war ; some men were as sour as a crab-apple, alarmed at a joke and ever ready to suspect impiety. Such an attitude would not commend the Faith ; "our purpose is not to force men to goodness but to win them". There were times when a spade ought to be called a spade but even this must be done in a Christlike manner. The basis of the Christian's conviction, in his view, was the glow and enthusiasm of an inner experience and he rejoiced that he had never subscribed to a creed and never would. He also held that never since the first century had the Church been brought so close to the mind of Christ, and this had been due to the fresh study of the Gospels (1896, 51-3). In these respects also he must have been somewhat disturbing to those who took a pride in the definite doctrinal position of the Presbyterian Church of Wales.

A transatlantic preacher who responded to the invitation of the Conference was Dr. Lorimer, a Scot who had emigrated to America and had become the Baptist minister of Tremont Temple in Boston. He spoke of the work of the Holy Spirit in guiding the Church into all truth, and yet it was the quest for truth by fallible human beings which led to denominational division ; "a divided Christendom is proof of the importance which the children of God attach to intellectual honesty". However, as they shared in a common exaltation of Christ they would draw nearer to each other. He did not think that the quest for truth was to be equated with an attempt to draw up agreed doctrinal formulae, the "iron cages of men's devices", nor did he think that the old creeds and formularies were as valuable as many supposed (1898, 11-7).

In 1901, Rev. P. T. Forsyth, D.D., Principal of Hackney College, London was the preacher. His posthumous fame has far outstripped his fame in his own day but his sermon at Merthyr Tydvil had all the elements of striking aphorism and paradox which have become familiar to all his subsequent readers. "The object of faith is not truth, but the truth, the last reality ; . . . we are not saved by believing truths but by trusting ourselves to Christ ; . . . we are not sanctified by seeing into truths but by living into Christ ; . . . we become real by contact with reality ; . . . the death of Christ was the judgement of all judgements ; . . . the evolution of history is an evolution of revolutions" (1901, 17-22).

In 1909 Rev. Dr. David Smith, Blairgowrie, and later of the Presbyterian College, Belfast, visited the Conference and his reflections on the Conference were of considerable interest as providing an external view of Welsh Presbyterianism. He said he was struck by the singing ; "until I heard your singing I never realised the power of song". He was also impressed by what he defined as the combination of evangelical piety and intellectual alacrity" which he had found among the younger ministers and which made them eager to interpret the old Faith to the mind of the new age (1909, 21).

In 1910 Rev. W. M. Clow, Glasgow, who later became a Professor in the Free Church College in Glasgow, said there was a noted improvement in common ethical standards though he admitted that not "all Christians wear the white flower of a blameless life". He held that the improvement could only be maintained if sustained by a grasp of sound doctrine (1910, 16-7). Like Smith he remarked upon "the marvellous singing with its volume and organlike solemnity", and upon the combination in the Conference of executive and scholarly ability and a happy reasonableness of mind (1910, 45-6).

In 1919 Rev. John A. Hutton, D.D., Glasgow, who was later to become editor of the *British Weekly* but who had already gained a reputation as preacher and lecturer, addressed the Conference. This was the first Conference since 1913 and the first since the Great War. Hutton's sermon was typical of the prosiness and indefiniteness which marked much of his writing and gave it the air of remoteness from current concerns. It has always been difficult to account for his reputation but he must have had a personal magnetism which gave to his spoken word a fire which cannot be caught from the written word. Yet there was one sentence which, though typical of Hutton's verbosity, did give a salutary warning to the Church : "Seducing voices assailed the Christian community, appealing to the Church to think less highly of itself, to abandon its supernatural speech, to come frankly down amongst men and mix with their ambitions, having a compassion even for their sins which was really nothing more than contempt for their possibilities,—voices which had then and have now but one intention, that we should remove the Cross, the rock of stumbling and offence from our testimony and from our demand" (1919, 5). Hutton also spoke on the prospects of Church Union in Scotland, and he said he took it as a basic truth that Christ was in His Church and was working in ways beyond human intelligence, even in ways that seemed contrary to human intelligence. He said that the idea of the unity of the Church was so evident to himself that "he did not argue with the man who was opposed to union, just as he did not argue with a man who did not believe in "God". He allowed that circumstances and timing would differ and that in Scotland the basic similarity of polity would make union more straightforward than in Wales, but the goal was the same (1913, 13-4).

The Conference Sermon in 1921 was delivered by the distinguished and stormy minister of King's Weigh House, London, Rev. W. E. Orchard, D.D. His sermon on the theme, "Worthy is the Lamb" (Rev. 5. v. 11), displayed the remarkable liturgical sense, verbal mastery, and social concern which attracted so many to hear him. Christian worship, in his view, must be full of penitence and obedience, and he applied this theme to his own post-war days when people found it difficult to confess their sins, and when there was also plenty to confess; they were living in an age whose hands were red with unrepented blood, whose banks were full of gold and whose barns full of grain, but which at the same time could watch millions starve. Orchard believed that this was an age which had barred the door upon God and "if God is going to effect anything with some of us He must be willing to take infinite pains" (1921, 4-10). Orchard also addressed the Conference on "the social implications of our great doctrines"; he held that the doctrine of the Trinity implied a social concern in the inmost recesses of reality, while the doctrines of the Incarnation and the Eucharist proclaimed the meeting of highest and lowest in God's purpose, and he found it significant that the word communion had the same root as the word communism (1921, 16-7).

Rev. J. R. Fleming, D.D., Secretary of the Presbyterian Alliance, visited the Conference in 1922 and he hoped that the forthcoming quadrennial conference of the Alliance to be held in Cardiff in 1925 would help to bring Welsh Presbyterianism more closely into the Presbyterian family. He said, "I do not think anything can compare with Welsh singing when you get it at its best" (1922, 7).

Mr. Basil Matthews, M.A., the noted missionary writer, visited the Conference in 1923 and his speech could equally well have been made in 1965 as a catalogue of the world's intractable problems. He said changes were taking place in the world; everything was in the crucible. All races were now inter-dependent. Primitive societies and ancient civilisations were both in the melting pot, and the spirit of self-determination was more rampant than co-operation. He was sure that the Christian missionary effort was in the centre of all effective reconstructive activity (1923, 29-32).

Rev. R. C. Gilie, D.C.L., from the Presbyterian Church of England, spoke in 1928 about the contemporary religious situation. There was a steadfast inner core of members in the churches but there was a prevailing mood of depression as hopes of revival faded. Special evangelistic campaigns had proved to be largely futile, and he took Belfast as an instance of a locality where there had been a considerable revival five or six years previously but from which there had been a scanty abiding harvest. This was all the more disappointing since the people of Northern Ireland were known to be more regular church-goers than the people of any other region in the British Isles, "unless Wales still holds the palm". He said that even successful campaigns made "no serious invasion of the ranks of the spiritually indifferent" and he added that he came to this conclusion reluctantly since he himself had been led to Christ in such a campaign (1928, 18).

Rev. A. D. Belden addressed the Conference in 1930. His presence was particularly appropriate since he was minister of Whitefield's Tabernacle and thus had a link with the early days of the Calvinistic Methodist movement. He spoke with his usual prophetic zeal and forecast a war within twenty-five years unless means were evolved to make war impossible. The world was flowing together and its people must either mingle or clash. The Church had failed to offer guidance to the troubled world. Whitefield had been able to make himself heard by 30,000, but now when radio gave to the Church the means of speaking to the planet it was down in the dumps like a lot of miserable sinners which in fact they were. The Church's message had failed to catch the ear of the world because it seemed too domestic compared with the power and glory unveiled by popular science.

The message was often presented as a technique of keeping in a good temper with life. Moreover, there was the moral failure displayed on the small scale by the personal sins of professedly religious people, and on the large scale by the failure to keep out of or to stop war or to bring industrial peace. The cure was deep and costly and would not be accomplished by "a fat-paid evangelist" filling a church (1930, 48-51).

Dr. Garfield Williams, Dean of Llandaff and later Dean of Manchester, was an invited speaker in 1930 ; he thus came on his own account rather than as an official delegate of his own Church. His address on the marks of a Christian life was warmly welcomed. He said that Christ could not fill himself into a life already filled with self, and the Church included many who were full of shrewd activity and full of their own importance, but they were not Christian (1930, 82).

Rev. Dr. H. H. Farmer, Westminster College, Cambridge, preached at the Llanidloes Conference in 1937 ; he said that the Church as he came across it was far from what it ought to be; it was divided, feeble, complacent and compromising, and ministers and laymen were more than a little dejected. He did not think this attitude was defensible for the very basis of discipleship was to be found in the Cross ; to join the Church was not to join a brilliant and successful institution or to share immediately in a triumphal procession but it involved sharing in the Cross. Jesus had said, "If I will that he tarry till I come, follow thou me" (1937, 12).

The Conferences were aware of the existing God-given unity of the Church and of the need to make it manifest in the world. Speakers often referred to the need for unity in impeccable words of aspiration, but they spoke in days when the thaw in denominational relations had just begun and when warm sentiments did not involve any immediate commitment. As aspiration must seek to move forward into commitment or else be proved an empty hope, the denominations in Wales are increasingly aware of the obstacles in the way of action ; the ideal often seems to be a receding vision.

Chapter V

EVANGELISM AND SOCIAL DUTY

THERE was general recognition of the Church's duty to evangelise and win the masses of the people. The Presbyterian outlook was largely shaped by the revivals which had occurred in Wales and in particular by the pioneering efforts of John Pugh who was the power behind the Forward Movement. At the very first Conference Pugh asserted that "the masses were the easiest people in the world to get at if the Gospel of Jesus Christ were only preached to them" (1889, 44). In 1893 Rev. J. Verrier Jones, Rhyl, said that while statistics showed that the Church was growing "we must go to the masses" for there was danger that "we live too much for our own personal progress" (1893, 11). Rev. Ellis Edwards, always the master of the vivid parallel, said that a Church which stayed at home was like a shell animal such as a crab or a lobster which had small walking powers but had exceptionally well-developed claws (1893, 11). Four years later he said the Church should be more concerned with the highways and hedges than with gowns and titles (1897, 61).

In 1897 Principal Prys of Trevecka spoke of the Forward Movement and regretted that like such movements as Christian Endeavour and the Temperance Movement it tended to become a sectional movement rather than a movement which had the backing of the whole Church. In his view, the Church seemed fated to become fossilised as a middle-class institution for which and by which the reality of the Cross was dimmed ; the Church had grown away from the masses and thereby had lost more than it could calculate (1897, 6-7). Nevertheless, the Forward Movement evangelists were well-placed to see the great work which had to be accomplished amid scenes of squalor ; "we are surrounded by a mass of dying humanity and to a large extent we are responsible for their well-being". One evangelist reported that "Swansea is in great need of the Gospel ; the depth of sin is appalling" (1895, 27-8). Evangelist Ray of Wrexham said in 1898 that there were hundreds in Wrexham whose ignorance, depravity and degradation were such that they would not listen to the Gospel being preached in the open-air at their own doors. Bad as were the cases he had seen in Cardiff "I have never beheld such wrecks of humanity as I have seen in the courts of Wrexham"; those who would help such people must be ready to reach out to them in their own hovels (1898, 94).

Mr. Edward Davies, J.P., Llandinam, a generous supporter of the Forward Movement, referred in 1895 to a recent Home Office report which showed the heavy incidence of drunkenness, violence and sexual crime in Glamorgan. He held that less than one half of the population ever went to church. The Presbyterian Church could only claim 22,000 members out of the 700,000 people in Glamorgan, and only 2,000 out of the 250,000 in Monmouth. He regarded the Forward Movement with its seventeen centres, 1,200 members and 6,000 adherents as a "star of hope" (1895, 94). In 1896 Rev. R. R. Roberts said that in South Wales the large majority of the population was indifferent or hostile to religion; people were pouring in from all parts and many of these were not civilised and were not Christians; all sorts of wickedness abounded among them but they could not be ignored for "they are your brothers and sisters" (1896, 78). In 1901 Dr. John Pugh referred to a *Daily Mail* report which said that Glamorgan was the black spot of the British Empire for crime and this was due to the arrival of wild spirits from all over the world (1901, 75).

Such accumulations of population were hotbeds of temptation for the young. Mr. G. P. Reynolds, Newport, said that the young working boy was in danger of becoming a city hooligan ready for any deed of mischief, and the middle-class boy was in danger of becoming "a young swell with a high collar and a cane lounging over bar counters talking flippant nonsense or worse to the attractive barmaid" (1905, 83).

The field for evangelism was ripe but there was considerable debate about the methods of evangelism. Rev. T. M. Green, Carmarthen, advocated the holding of two types of service, one for the members whom he classed as God's own people, the other for those who were as yet only adherents or still outsiders, but Rev. R. H. Morgan, Menai Bridge, said that such a division would lead to Pharisaism among the members and would further encourage an ennervating emotionalism which he found detrimental to true religion (1889, 42-3). In 1901 Seth Joshua, Pugh's colleague in leading the Forward Movement, said that of late the Church had been giving an undue prominence to ethics with a strong admixture of socialism but the multitudes remained obstinately outside the churches; he also said there was need for a deep and continuing compassion for the souls of men and he pilloried the spasmodic and seasonal work of the Church as if it were inconvenient for the Almighty to save a soul in the summer-time which was becoming an ecclesiastical close season (1901, 80-1).

However, there were those who pointed out that the very existence of the English-speaking churches in the Connexion was proof of the missionary effort of many in the Welsh-speaking churches who in the face of great difficulties had sought to provide churches for those who could only speak English.

Indeed the whole work of the Connexion was carried on amid difficulties. In 1899 Rev. J. Glyn Davies spoke of obstacles in the way of English speaking churches in the rural areas ; because of the tyrannous power of the State Church as wielded by the squire and the parson and also because of the stubborn Welsh adherence to their language many members drifted to the towns ; their financial resources were also very slender. Churches in the towns profited by this inflow from the rural areas but the gains were counterbalanced by losses due to unbelief, rationalism, secularism and indifference ; "our religious life is weakened and it as much as we can do to hold on". There were, said Davies, no resources for further advance and he saw an urgent need for Christian unity ; "if the Church of England, so pitiably proud, will stand aloof, why cannot the Free Churches unite ?" "Can we not rise in our one faith and set against these drainings of power the bankings of our common Christianity and our common humanity ?" (1899, 72-73). In 1901 Rev. J. Williams, B.A., Dolgelly, said there were still 800,000 in Wales who never attended any religious service and who would not be won by a church torn by sectarian divisions (1901, 79).

At the turn of the century Wales was clearly not a land of predominantly church-going people. In 1894 Dr. Ebenezer Davies, the Medical Officer of Health for Swansea and later to be President of the Conference, said that an increasing proportion of the people had no church connection. Among the wealthier classes many spent Sunday morning in social entertainment and on intellectual pursuits while the humbler classes went on excursions by rail, road or steamboat. In his opinion, those who went to Church did so as a duty rather than as a joyful observance (1894, 30).

Disregard of the Christian observance of Sunday was noted in 1900 by Rev. A. J. Jenkins who later became the Presbyterian minister of Enniskillen in Ireland. He listed some recent instances of such desecration ; a crowd had gone to the Strand Theatre in London to see the play "Candida" by George Bernard Shaw and there had been no protest in the London papers ; Cardiff barmaids and barmen held their sports at Barry and followed this by a supper and prize-giving in a hotel, once again without protest ; there had also been cricket matches, card parties, lawn tennis matches, musical at-homes, theatricals, feasting, visiting, pleasure-tripping, and Sunday labour ; all these were signs that "a latitudinarian spirit was abroad" (1900, 48). The remedy, in Jenkins' view, was not a withdrawal to the rigours of the Jewish Sabbath which had been for ever superseded by Christ. Religious fervour was not necessarily present amid funereal gloom and there was no piety in cold mutton on the Sabbath. "Rules, regulations and petty observance have had their day and must cease to be". The day was intended to be a day of rest and joy and its proper observance was made almost impossible by late hours on Saturday by which shop-assistants were made weary and worn and listless on the Lord's Day (1900, 48). In 1904 Mr. H. H. Meyler, M.A., Machynlleth, noted that zeal for Sabbath observance could accompany dishonourable dealing of man with man and in this way Christ was dishonoured and his day brought into disrespect (1904, 81). In 1905 Rev. C. J. Lewis, Barry, spoke with unusual liberality on the theological warrant for the observance of Sunday. It was not a continuation of the Jewish Sabbath ; it was the Lord's Day and its main note was not one of rest but of worship. He pointed out that the early Christians had had to work on Sunday and their concern was not to make time for rest but for worship. However, he thought that the churches had gone too far from the idea of rest and had so filled up the day with a round of activities that there was no time for rest (1905, 69-70). Mr. G. Cromar, C.C., J.P., Rossett, also deplored the decline in reverence for Sunday and attributed this to the decay of worship and discipline in the home as well as to the increasing commercialisation of the day, an instance of which was the recent gathering of nineteen thousand sieves of strawberries at Wisbech on a Sunday (1905, 68). Rev. Joseph Evans said that in Rhyl and Llandudno "the sanctity of the Sabbath" had been largely abolished (1905, 65). Rev. J. Verrier Jones took up Meyler's earlier point and said that the Church's own programme of services, meetings and schools had in part broken up the Sunday in the home. Mothers were prone to misuse the day by being "more eager to deck out their children's bodies in gay attire than to array heir souls in the beauteous garments of simplicity and truth". In this way, even among "the sweet domesticities of home" there was implanted a desire for the tyrannous pleasures of the world". This led to a general decline in conduct and Jones saw omens of further decline in the crowds of young men and boys on the streets on Sabbath evenings "with bold looks and ribald words on their lips" as well as girls who "sully their modesty by permitting themselves to be hustled and insulted by these young mannikins of the street" (1905, 65-6).

This persisting tone of reproof sounds somewhat strange coming as it did on the morrow of the 1904 Revival. At the 1905 Conference in Penarth a Free Church Council deputation did indeed remark on "the recent Pentecostal blessing" when thousands had been converted and in which all denominations had shared" (1905, 9). Mr. Augustus Lewis, the retiring President, also referred to the tokens of Divine Presence during the year when between eight and ten thousand members had been added to the Presbyterian Church of Wales but he also dispelled any thought that all Wales had been swept into the churches and he indicted the coldness and carelessness of much Church life (1905, 22-3). Rev. J. M. Saunders, M.A., Swansea, said that the Revival had changed the face of the land and the life of the churches; there had been a renewal among nominal members and an influx of converts. Nevertheless, he too saw perils ahead and he was troubled over the apathy of many ministers who lagged behind their people in welcoming the Revival (1905, 60). Dr. Cynddylan Jones gave a cautious estimate of the value of the Revival. He said that many had been swept into the churches but many had also been swept out whose inconsistent lives could not endure the breath of awakened zeal. He also noted that there had been an outbreak of censoriousness among converts who looked with a critical eye upon any whose long-standing faith was less effusive than their own; "I object to the excitement of the Revival now going on in Wales". Dr. Jones held that a reheated excitement was not desirable; he preferred a reheated glow rather than a blaze and held that such a glow would be none the less genuine witness to the presence of the Holy Spirit. On the whole, however, he welcomed the Revival which had broken the monotony of Church life and even if the young converts were to outrun the old "we will try to follow to be witnesses of the resurrection life in Jesus Christ" (1905, 63-4).

Great as were the results of the Revival there remained hosts of people untouched by the Church. Rev. J. Morgan Jones, Cardiff, spoke of the need for a Christianity aggressive against sin. He drew a somewhat idyllic picture of a past when "all the people" attended Church and read the Bible in their homes and he compared this with his own time when Monmouth and Glamorgan was over-run by an alien population with depraved habits and among whom the Church had to work (1909, 67-8). Rev. John Hughes, M.A., the Moderator-elect of the General Assembly, told the Conference in 1910 that the Free Churches were specially fitted for making contact with the people and said they had none of the liabilities of the Anglican clergy who were ministers of a Church which for centuries had been the State Church and was "the richest in the world". Too many Anglican clergy were of "the degenerate type of ecclesiastic as construed in the light of a state Church whose policy and ecclesiasticism is formed more in the interests of the State than the necessities of the Church". Nevertheless, great things could be achieved if all the Churches could combine in the interests of even religious education and temperance reform (1910, 74-8). However, Rev. J. Morgan Jones, M.A., Merthyr, was more realistic when he said that even with roots among the common people the Free Churches were not reaching the masses of the people especially in the towns and industrial areas. Jones also held that the industrial age was producing a new type of man who was not interested in Christian doctrine however adapted and revised. The new man had been reared in hard circumstances and was pragmatic and sceptical and had no reverence, delicacy, trustfulness or refinement. Such men had no place for the normal activities of the Church and he asserted that in 1906 in one town alone 10,000 men had severed their connection with any church. Many, in his view, assumed that the Gospel as they had known it was unable to cope with the new situation and they regarded the Church as discredited because it had not lifted up its voice against the unrighteousness which lay behind slum dwellings and wages as low as 22 pence for an 11 hour day (1910, 78-82).

Prof. T. A. Levi, Aberystwyth, admitted a gap between the Church and the masses but saw it in a different light. He said there was a natural dignity about the working man which resented any hint of condescension or patronage and he accused the Church of withdrawing from the service of the people. He was not worried if churches of 1000 were reduced to churches of 100 so long as the remnant proved that it really cared for people. The Church ought to bring education to the people but this was not to be equated as it was in Cardiganshire with a university degree; he wondered why the Church was "so easily gulled by degrees" because the "educated man is the man who acts, thinks and speaks as a man who loves his fellowmen and is willing to serve them". By this standard some working men were more educated than members of a university. Levi also held that division was fostered by social segregation; "the caste system in India is nothing to the caste system of England". Wages were such as to make some into slaves to enrich others, and yet there were those who held that any increase in wages would breed avarice; those who said this were the descendants of those who used to pay preachers sixpence a Sunday. Again, landlords owned the land and it was futile for the people to sing "Land of my fatners"; forty million people had no legal right to exist and had no stake in the land. Levi held there was a case for nationalisation of land which was too sacred to be left for speculation. Moreover, disease ravaged the land and on tombstones it was often stated that God called the dead; "He never did". Levi said that the public-house, the workhouse and the gaol needed to be levelled to the ground (1910, 83-5).

Many speakers felt that the Church was hindered by indifference rather than by active hostility. Rev. J. H. Owen, Pembroke, saw this indifference in various guises ranging from fashionable formalism through periods of hypocondria between religious excitements to cynical patronage of Christ and Christianity. All these, in his view, sprung in part from decadent preaching, poor music, class distinctions within the Church, but basically they were due to the lure of luxuries and amusements which followed in the wake of prosperity (1902, 29-30). Rev. Evan Evans, Arddleen, also laid much of the blame upon the forces of wealth and culture (1902, 36). Mr. John Owens, Llandinam, attributed indifference to the current depreciation of the supernatural in religion, to the laxity with which admission and discipline in the Church were administered, and the inadequate emphasis placed upon truth, obedience, duty and kindness in the teaching of the young (1902, 32). Rev. Arthur Wynne Thomas, Aberystwyth, said people were interested in everything but not deeply committed to anything. Education had stressed cleverness rather than character and had produced men who were cleverer but not necessarily better than their fathers. Thomas said that bigotry and intolerance were now frowned upon but "it is the men who take extreme views of things that have made history in the past" (1902, 42-3). In 1911 the retiring President, Alderman S. N. Jones, spoke of "the majority of our members" who attended church only once on Sunday or even less if they happened to be week-ending, and he said there was lack of enthusiasm, lack of a sense of sacrifice, lack of well-attended prayer-meetings (1911, 30-3). In 1920 Rev. William Mendus said laziness was the greatest blight on the Church (1920, 4).

The answer to indifference in the opinion of many speakers was the christianisation of Christians. For example, in 1925 Rev. R. G. Jones, West Kirby, said that Sabbath desecration would not be stopped by eloquent sermons on the Fourth Commandment but by a proper observance of the day by Christians themselves (1925, 30). Rev. E. Cynolwyn Pugh, B.A., whose own remarkable story is told in his autobiography, *Ei Ffanffer ei Hun*, told the same Conference that he discerned signs of awakening in the Church. He himself owed a great debt to the 1904 Revival and he said that any true religion must generate emotion though he was not thinking of a mere repetition of 1859 or 1904; he saw signs of life in such movements as C.O.P.E.C. and the S.V.M.U. through which a recent wave of 3,000 volunteers had been drawn into the missionary work of the Church. Pugh held that people needed to be presented with an intelligent conception of a moral God somewhat different from the hard being so often presented by Calvinism. He held that people needed to be galvanised rather than Calvinised (1925, 31-5). Rev. John Roberts, Wrexham spoke in, his valedictory presidential address in 1933 of the apathy caused by the natural perversity of human nature, the misunderstanding of scientific knowledge and the general secular spirit, but he also said there was a reaction against a zeal which was not according to knowledge and which antagonised many by a narrow denominational outlook (1933, 17-22).

There were also numerous indications that evangelism could be carried out through a diligent Christian life and through a vital opposition to social evils. In 1910 Rev. A. Wynne Thomas, Swansea, said that while the round of Church services and meetings was of great importance this activity was not necessarily more religious than work in the shop, the office, the bank, the council, the House of Commons, and, "if you like, even for the House of Lords" (1910, 62-3).

Many speakers thought the Church would not be heeded until its conscience was awake to many things then tolerated such as commercial morality, the drink trade, excessive luxury, the crass selfishness lying behind much conventional virtue (1913, 18-9).

As early as 1892 Ellis Edwards spoke of the ravages caused by drink and commended recent legislation which had enabled the authorities in such cities as Cardiff and Liverpool to curtail much intemperance. He was confident that if the Church demanded greater control of the licensed trade it would be granted but he also held that the Church's duty went beyond agitation and condemnation. "Christian Churches must provide public-houses without drink or where the sale of drink was strictly limited or guarded"; he referred to cocoa rooms set up by the churches in Liverpool (1892, 19). Mr. S. N. Jones, Abertillery, said that churches ought to open up vestries as places of shelter and as alternatives to the public houses (1892, 25). Rev. R. H. Lundie, D.D., Liverpool, told how 22 licences had been revoked in Liverpool and said there was need to press on for Sunday closing, for closing at 10 p.m. on weekdays and at 9 p.m. on Saturdays (1892, 19). Mr. J. H. Roberts, M.P., who was later to be ennobled as Lord Clwyd and also to become the President of the Conference and the first layman to become Moderator of the General Assembly, was hopeful of reform since thirty-one out of the thirty-four Welsh M.P.s were pledged to measures of reform, and despite the vast drink bill he was confident that "Wales was a temperate nation" (1892, 19).

In 1894 Mrs. Gwyneth Vaughan said that the Church ought to be the great Temperance Society campaigning for the restraint of a licensed trade which had a license to make drunkards (1894, 58).

Alderman J. Jones Griffiths, Penygraig, a notable public figure in the Rhondda, said that one of the greatest obstacles to an effective curb on the drink traffic was public indifference even to the fate of young men who were being drawn into the vortex and were slipping down to a drunken doom. The Church's own record, in his view, was far from what it ought to be; there was a type of deacon who sat as "the smug Pharisee in his capacious armchair under the pulpit ejaculating hollow assent to truth enunciated thereform" and yet could also sell drink and so provide a means of ruin for a weaker brother; moreover, churches and chapels which received donations from brewers and publicans were culpable, for such gifts were nought but hush-money to salve unquiet consciences; there were also decent folk, lay and clerical, whose names appeared on the shareholders' lists of the great brewing concerns (1896, 79-80). Rev. John Pugh also thought that members and deacons with shares in breweries and distilleries were not likely to be zealous to curb the liquor traffic (1898, 62). In 1900 Rev. Thomas Jones, Rhostyllen, said that the dreadful consequences of intemperance were such that it was the "plain duty of everyman to avoid even the risk of acquiring the craving for drink" ; all drunkards had started as moderate drinkers and there was no remedy other than total abstinence. Christ had given a command to pluck out every cause of offence (1900, 49).

In 1901 Rev. T. G. Owen, M.A., Liverpool, referred to a Free Church target of one million total abstinence pledges within one year and said that this was not impossible in the light of Father Matthew's Irish campaign which had secured 250,000 pledges in one month. The need for drastic action was seen in the trail of lives ruined by drink and in the current annual expenditure of £150,000,000 in Britain alone upon drink. He said that no arguments could disprove that the number of public-houses and of drunkards went hand in hand. In Scotland Rd. in Liverpool there were fifty-six public-houses but none in Parliament Fields ; for every crime committed in Parliament fields there were hundreds on Scotland Road. He claimed that all the Labour Members of Parliament were teetotallers (1901, 51-3). Rev. Arthur Wynne Thomas, Aberystwyth, said that though all the arguments against the drink traffic were well-known they were ineffective since there was "no conviction of its tremendous evil" (1901, 43). Nevertheless, Rev. J. Glyn Davies could call in 1903 for a greater aggressiveness in exposing the wealth of the drink trade and its power in public affairs and also the social position accorded to the princes of the traffic. When he considered the vast amount of drinking, albeit on a moderate scale, in connection with commercial bargains and social functions, even in the homes of professing Christians and church officers, he thought it was high time for every minister to have clean hands and every deacon to have clean lips (1902, 46). In 1909 Rev. W. Wynne Davies, Bangor, said that intemperance was the greatest evil in the land and the source of more misery than squalor, pauperism, murder and all other vices combined. In 1908 there had been 200,000 cases of drunkenness before the courts, and even allowing for a slight decline in the annual amount consumed the position was only back to where it was twenty years previously, and Davies noted a new factor in the increasing number of women involved in drinking. The press also remained in sympathy with the "nefarious habit" (1909, 98-9). Rev. T. G. Owen, M.A., returned to the theme in 1912 in his retiring presidential address and said that if it remained impossible to drive drink out of the world the Church should at least drive it out of its own life and he pled with the Association in the North to follow the example of the South and enforce the Connexional policy that ministers and elders should be teetotallers (1912, 33-4). This plea was renewed in 1921 by Mr. John Owens, J.P., Chester, who held there was urgent need for such a witness against a trade which had never been more flourishing. Some Presbyteries, he said, had already begun to implement the policy in the North and though it could not be made retrospective Owens appealed to those already in office to make a voluntary vow of abstinence and for the sake of others give up what was for them no more than "a trifling pleasant vice" (1921, 61-2).

Serious as were the ravages of drunkenness it was clearly not looked upon as the only social evil. Indeed, there were those who regarded the social structure as so unfair as to drive men to seek an escape in drink. In 1894 Mr. J. H. Lewis, M.P., said that England had become a paradise for the wealthy and was in danger of becoming a purgatory for the poor. The Church had a duty to be the champion of the poor, the needy and the afflicted, and he regarded it as a failure on the Church's part that the only place of recreation in many villages was the public-house (1894, 53).

Mrs. Gwyneth Vaughan, London, declared in 1894 that squalor, sweated-labour, infant mortality and the degradation of barmaids were evils which ought not to exist and the Christian ought to be in the battle for social betterment since Christ was the greatest social reformer ever known (1894, 58).

Moreover, many people were made poor so as to enrich the rich. Dr. Owen Morris, M.D., Birkenhead, said that Christians had so emphasised the glories of the life to come that they had neglected the present world and had allowed the poor to sink into a condition which was a "disgrace to Christendom". Thousands were annually launched into eternity to give larger dividends to investors (1898, 62). This desire for wealth was at the root of gambling. Rev. J. R. Davies, Swansea, took issue with a statement of the Anglican, Rev. J. E. C. Welldon, later to become a bishop and Dean of Durham, that gambling was only wrong when it became detrimental to other aspects of life.

Davies preferred the view of Hugh Price Hughes that gambling was sinful whether the amount was threepence or £1,000 (1898, 59-60).

In 1901 Mr. Keir Hardie, M.P. addressed the Conference. *Y Goleuad* praised the Conference committee for its courage in inviting so colourful a figure whose advent to Parliament as the first Labour M.P. had aroused controversy and apprehension.[2] He attacked the social evils of the time and asserted that the state of society was unworthy of twenty centuries of Christian effort. In his view the living conditions of the people had deteriorated in the nineteenth century. He accused the liquor traffic of causing appalling harm to the community. He doubted the value of local option for which many ministers had been pressing; it was precisely the areas which most needed control which would be the least likely to vote for any restraint. He also mentioned a Scottish referendum to decide whether there should be total suppression of public-houses, reduction to a quota in proportion to the population, or public management of the trade. He allowed that many were alarmed at any public responsibility for the trade but he thought that this method might bring the matter home to citizens and move them to clean up a trade for whose management they were responsible. As for gambling he thought it was a worse blight upon the nation than even drink and, like many speakers, he classed stock exchange transactions as gambling practices to be condemned. Moreover, there was the whole structure of society which was run for profit and in the process workers were being ruined. He saw socialism as the only hope of reform (1901, 49-51). Rev. R. G. Jones, Egremont, also held that a shilling on a horse and fortunes on the Stock Exchange were both forms of gambling (1902, 70). In 1909 Mr. E. P. Lewis, Shrewsbury, held that gambling had now become a general menace. Hitherto rich men, among whom Lewis named the Duke of Devonshire, had chosen to squander their resources in gambling and Calvinistic Methodists could do little to restrain such men who were "educated and intelligent". Gambling had now become deeply rooted in the whole structure of society; politicians, workers, servants, police, post-office workers, women and children were all involved in gambling. Lotteries, press competitions and card games were widespread and an army of book makers reaped £5 million yearly from the public. He also thought that many stock exchange transactions were tainted with gambling and he quoted Horatio Bottomley for the view that 90% of such transactions were purely gambling affairs. Later events would not encourage a belief in Bottomley's reliability. Lewis thought there was a decline of lotteries at Chapel Bazaars and this makes a significant remark upon the vaunted purity of church life in earlier times (1909, 91-3). Lewis thought the time was ripe for a campaign to secure the reform of the betting laws and the abolition of the professional betting man. In his opinion the Churches were apathetic and had shown no response to the call of the Free Church Federation in 1902 for a concerted campaign against gambling. Consciences were becoming hardened and thus were unaware of the evil of the Turf "which is a vast engine of national and individual demoralization" and led to a loss of money, health, nerve and character (1909, 94-5).

Bad housing was also a source of anxiety. In 1903 Mr. Timothy Davies, a London Councillor, said that unless people could be removed from the slums they could not get out of their old habits (1903, 67). He was supported by Mr. Evan Evans, Aberystwyth, in his assertion that as few as two or three determined men on a town council could do incalculable good in getting action to improve housing (1903, 67, 73). Mr. Evans said that three quarters of the population lived in towns and often in poor conditions with a poor supply of light, air, and water. He held that 120,000 deaths could be prevented each year if conditions were improved, and he said that half of the children who died under five years of age were the victims of unhealthy houses and imperfect sanitation. Such conditions were also detrimental to intellectual, social and moral growth. Evans said that many Acts relating to drainage, water, housing, factories, libraries, and other social amenities had been passed but their effective application had been hindered by the procrastination of local councils which were hesitant to increase the burden of rates, but such a burden was part of the citizen's Christian duty (1903, 73). Evans' son, Mr. Ernest Evans, B.A., LL.B., returned to the problem in 1913 and pointed out the stark inequalities in society ; at one extreme, £100 could be spent for a night's entertainment while at the other extreme a child could be dying of starvation in the slums ; or, in another case, the wealth of the Empire could be displayed in a procession in Whitehall while at the same time poor people could be huddled for shelter under the arches of a nearby bridge (1913, 45).

Behind this social concern there was the conviction that the Church should be the home of all classes and ought to avoid temptations to become either a synagogue for the rich or a club for the poor (1901, 55). Rev. Evan Evans, Arddleen, said that the old relationship between master and serf had been succeeded by the new relationship of the impersonal syndicate and the industrial worker ; the worker often felt he had no prospect of advancement and suspected that the Church was on the side of capital. He felt that the war of the future would be between capital and labour and it was time the Church insisted on the obligations of the owners of wealth (1902, 36). Rev. R. G. Jones, Egremont, said that there were mutual obligations between employers and workers. Workers ought to get a fair day's wage for a fair day's work (1903, 70). Mr. J. R. Davies, J.P., in his retiring address as President in 1902 thought that many business men were not driven primarily by the lust for gold ; they were ready to mix with all races and to trust one another and indeed could teach the Church to be ready to try fresh methods in its work (1902, 17).

In 1906 Rev. J. Talog Davies, Beaufort, sketched the growth of the industrial society and said that workmen were at the mercy of forces they could not control. As yet, the power of Trade Unions was limited. Glaring inequalities persisted. A dinner in the Savoy could cost £80 for each guest while in its shadow men and women were dying of starvation. God called no man to idleness and no man ought to be content in a position to which God had not called him. Unless the Church had become bankrupt it surely had something to say about conditions where men were unemployed and seemingly unemployable. The Church's task was not to save an élite but to save society by means of the elect. When the Conference applauded Davies' remarks he said that the applause would need to be accompanied by much heart-searching for there were churches out of which working men were frozen and where Jesus himself would not be welcome (1906, 44-5). Puleston Jones said that Protestants were prone to forget the doctrine of the Incarnation which implied God's concern for all that was necessary for the life of man (1906, 48). Arthur Henderson, the noted Socialist pioneer, told the Conference that he welcomed the Church's interest in the social needs of the people. He said that in the past parsons had tended to support social policies only after they had become popular. Indeed there were, in his view, still some in the Church who felt absolved from any concern with social affairs because they were not citizens of this world but those who said so were often remote from the conditions under which many have had to live, and there were still grim housing conditions; he estimated that in the whole country between eleven and twelve millions were on the verge of starvation. Moreover, he felt that many charitable activities were palliatives which covered over the immensity of the need and deadened the public conscience. Henderson felt that while the Church's interest in social conditions had increased the Churches were being injured by the "miserable representation of Christianity that is being put before the people" (1906, 49-51).

The Great War caused an enormous social upheaval with a new sense of the evil of class distinction. To the old social evils were now added fresh class hatreds. In 1920 there were many references to class-hatred, pleasure-seeking, money-grabbing, drunkenness, immorality, suicides and murders. Mr. S. Glynne Jones, B.A., O.B.E., said that the Church had acquiesced in the drift of society from its spiritual basis; poverty, suffering, want, greed and extravagance were sapping the vitals of the nation which was also held in the grip of impurity and intemperance. Jones said that when the war was over there was strong pressure to reduce the price of beer but the price of milk was left to the processes of unending conferences. In a recent influenza epidemic Sunday Schools had had to close but cinemas remained open. Not nearly enough had been done for slum-clearance though the Ministry of Health had acted creditably in holding up the building of forty-two cinemas so that the labour and material should be devoted to housing (1920, 15-17).

The comradeship of the trenches had broken down many barriers and when the soldiers returned they were aware as never before of the divisions of society, and there were thus fresh grounds for strife. Rev. J. H. Howard said that the masses were educated as never before and they now had the vote but they would not necessarily be bound by constitutional methods, and just at the time when their power was increasing the Churches were in decreasing contact with these awakening masses. Moreover, in his view, it was a weakness that Anglicans were so closely linked to Conservatism, and Non-conformists to Liberalism; it would only increase the weakness if Non-conformists switched to Labour. The Church's teaching ought to be the dynamic in all classes. Both capital and labour needed to be pointed to new ways of service. There was need of a new spirit of equality, though not an equality in the gutter but as high as the throne so that the pauper would be raised from the dust. Howard of course realised there would be no simple solution; the Co-operative method was good but it did not get rid of strikes; profit-sharing was good but it did not banish unemployment; nationalisation was difficult to reconcile with a man's right to withdraw his labour (1920, 32-6).

In a Conference sermon in 1933 Rev. M. Watcyn Williams said that the message of service seemed a mockery to those millions who were unemployed and so felt they were on the scrap-heap. Others were deaf to the call of service since they had devoted themselves to drink, drugs, betting, gambling and hectic pleasures. Others were members of the Church but for them their religion was not a call to service but a sacramental dope which substituted the Church for Christ and creed for the character which only the spirit can produce (1933, 10-12).

Many speakers from the earliest Conferences were aware of the damage done to human bodies, minds and characters by the inequalities produced by the prevailing economic system and the deep social malaise. They also realised that much could be done to counteract these injustices and ills by political action. Such action by itself would not solve all human problems but it was vital that such action should be recognised as an important social influence. If any members of the Conferences thought the Church should not interfere in social and political issues they were not vocal in the Conferences. Rev. Griffith Ellis, M.A., Bootle,[3] speaking in 1895, said the Church had a duty to examine the relation of capital and labour, luxury and want, wealth and poverty, peace and war, trade and commerce. Hesitation to pronounce upon these topics ought not to be because of cowardice but only because of "the difficulty to seize intelligently all the conditions of the problems that are pressing forward for solution" (1895, 31). He proceeded to set forth what he regarded as the basic truths, namely, the recognition that both the individual and society had rights and duties, and he saw some danger in recent legislation which tended to socialism and perhaps unduly restrained the individual, but the danger could be avoided if it were recognised that man's basic needs were spiritual and involved a total salvation of spirit, soul, and body, and of environment. Ellis regarded the regeneration of man himself as a pre-requisite for enduring social reform; indeed, "much of the poverty of our land is due to the habits of our people and not to the economic conditions under which they live". Reform enforced by legislation was less valuable than voluntary improvement by people themselves. If people were to decide to reduce what they spent on drink from £140 million to £100 million the money saved could be spent on necessities and the ensuing boom in trade would wipe out all unemployment. Mr. George Brown has recently pointed out that if there is not voluntary restraint then compulsion would have to be used. Ellis would probably have shrunk from this as he held that property was an inalienable right of the individual. He held that the pulpit was the place to proclaim principles which people would have to apply for themselves; ministers were not obliged to enunciate social schemes (1895, 32-3). However, the gap between principles and practical schemes could be very narrow as was evident in a speech by Rev. R. R. Roberts, Aberdare, when he said the Church had a duty to expose social ills and to seek a remedy. The laissez-faire solution was no solution. The Church had a duty to follow the example of the Early Church where the "highest spiritual rapture was accompanied by the most mathematical socialism"; the impassable gulfs in society were an offence to the "royal brotherhood to which the Cross has elevated men" and it was futile to expect spiritual culture while thousands are "sunk in the scale through poverty, crime and drunkenness"; to offer them only a glorious hereafter seems "a tale to mock their present misery"; God intended the improvement of the whole of manhood. Roberts said there were men loud in insisting that concern for human environment should not distract the Church from saving souls but who were also eager to build "chapels with ventilation, space, pews with receding backs and cushions too" (1895, 34-5). These points were lucidly reinforced by Mr. Owen Owen, M.A., J.P., Master of Oswestry High School, who held that Christ's picture of the final judgement and the tests to be applied gave ample warrant to his followers to "plunge into the seething vortex of social politics" (1895, 36). In 1897 he also said there was need of missions to the rich, the aristocracy, and the government who were all "so alert to act where the rights of property are concerned and so slow to act where the rights of men are at stake" (1897, 86A). Even seventy years later many are perplexed by the disparity between sentences for crimes against property and crimes against persons. Prof. Ellis Edwards gave a firm picture of the Church's duty in social matters; "a Christian cannot live except as he lives for others". Christians had to be socialists, and Christianity was the only socialism. All men were brothers to the whole world, and no man could be saved who made no effort to save others ; people were saved as they sought to save others. Christianity was not an insurance society for cowards who looked after their own skins and nothing else. Edwards then castigated those who made fortunes by tricky business methods such as adulterated goods, poor wares and underselling ; he declared that "no Christian man will allow unsanitary conditions, poor wages, destitution, poverty ; if an employer thrives on such, 'tis robbery" (1895, 39). In 1897 Edwards re-emphasised his points and said the basic human concern should be for others, customers and employees, as well as for oneself. He did not think it necessary that there should be a renunciation of wealth but a proper use of it to help others with wisdom and consideration ; it was preferable to help others to earn their own livelihood than to shower them with riches which would relieve them of all necessity to labour (1897, 83A). Rev. J. Morgan Jones, Merthyr, said it was particularly necessary for Celts to remember the inseparable links between religion and morality ; they were addicted to enthusiasm and idealism and mysticism, and among the Welsh there were those who disparaged morality in the supposed interests of religion ; indeed, "a man is called a heretic nowadays if he insists that morality and religion are one". Jones was aware that honesty was more than a prudential "best policy" and was an indispensable condition of inward character (1900, 51-2).

In 1905 Rev. R. R. Roberts returned to the theme and held that only a Free Church could speak with the necessary directness to society. An established Church was muzzled ; its representatives went to solemn banquets and drank toasts to the link between Church and State and in so doing made the Church "a poetic background, an aesthetic fringe, or pious anachronism" but if a church is truly a church it must be free to judge the state. Roberts held that the whole social structure was weighted in favour of property rather than persons so that a person who set fire to a haystack would be more severely punished than a man who kicked his wife downstairs. Members of Parliament were usually linked to property whether in the form of land, capital, ships, coal, or beer. It was time that voices such as those of Dr. John Clifford, Dr. Barnardo, General Booth, and the Welsh revivalist, Evan Roberts were heard in Parliament (1905, 98—100).

In 1908 Rev. T. C. Jones, Penarth, said that while the New Testament laid more emphasis upon men than upon their circumstances, Christ had never treated lightly the pains and diseases which afflicted people, and so the Church could not ignore the poverty which afflicted people in the twentieth century in Britain, "the richest country in the world". To solve this problem it might be necessary to break monopolies and to nationalise the means of production and distribution (1908, 57-9). Sir J. Herbert Lewis, M.P., said there would have been no problem to solve if the Church had obeyed the command to bear one another's burdens (1908, 55-6). Rev. T. G. Owen, M.A., Liverpool, also took the view that many who were Socialists had been driven from the Church by the inconsistent conduct of Christians. He said that even allowing for sickness, and drunkenness as causes of unemployment fifty-five per cent of the unemployed were genuine cases of unwanted labour. Christians, in his view, ought not to allow such tyranny to continue (1908, 63-69).

A view somewhat contrary to the prevailing opinion in the Conferences was put forward by Mrs. J. M. Saunders, Pencoed, in 1910. She said it was a mistake to think that all the poor were miserable. Indeed, in her view, "half the miseries of life arise out of our attempt to force ourselves out of the position into which God has placed us, or to our refusal to adjust ourselves to our social environment". She said that slum-dwellers were not a homogenous group. There were the aristocrats of the slums who were people of high morals and honest conduct and who despised the crudity of drunkenness, and these were difficult to win for Christ since they took the view that they were not behaving badly and could not be expected to do better. There were also the lifelong denizens of the slums who were miserable and hopeless and to whom the Gospel came as good news. There were also those who had sunk from affluence to the slums and whose shame and remorse were pitiable and who were almost impossible to claim for Christ. The slum-dwellers had therefore to be seen as individuals and could not be won by any impersonal social scheme (1910, 60-62).

Rev. John Edwards, Wrexham, spoke of social evils in his valedictory address as President in 1931. He said that the revolting spectacle of public drunkenness had almost disappeared and yet during the previous year the amount spent on drink had mounted to £277 million, an average of £6/4/0 by each person and that at a time of industrial depression. He also referred to prevalent betting and gambling and the deplorable desecration of the Lord's Day (1931, 19-20).

All the Conferences produced speakers well aware of the sins and injustices prevalent in Welsh society and at the same time conscious of the duty of the Church to all, even the worst.

Chapter VI

THE CHURCH AND POLITICS

THE political life of the period could not but be reflected in the Conferences. At home there were problems connected with education and establishment which had strong political overtones. Moreover, many leading laymen were Liberal politicians who tended to look with a Gladstonian eye upon world affairs. However, there was a public apathy to politics which disturbed political parties then as now, and also a tendency to make large promises at election times. In 1894, Rev. John Watson, a minister of the Presbyterian Church of England and better known as the novelist Ian Maclaren, told the Conference that it was shameful to see politicians promising "material boon which they knew perfectly well could never be given" (1894, 56). Alderman Jones Griffiths regretted that many quiet people did not vote when they had the opportunity and thus left the field open to scoundrels (1896, 80).

In 1899 the repercussions of the Dreyfus affair were felt in the Conference as well as anxiety about British policy in Africa. The Dreyfus affair caused particular alarm for it was felt to reveal Roman Catholic interference in politics. It seemed to many that the Roman Catholic Church in France had sanctioned falsehood and duplicity so as to discredit its critics. Mr. Morgan Thomas, Cardiff, took the occasion to denounce a "so-called Church" which ignored the cry for justice and could plot for the life of the innocent and could make it a virtue to bear false witness. Thomas said the obvious lesson for Britain was to resist the growth of "modern popes" in the parishes of the country, a reference not only to Roman Catholic expansion but to Anglo-Catholic infiltration into the Church of England. In Africa, the career of Cecil Rhodes was reaching its controversial climax. Rev. H. Barrow Williams, Llanidloes, referred with scorn to Joseph Chamberlain's assertion that Rhodes was "in his personal character worthy" ; this was to assume that a man could be personally worthy quite apart from his public conduct. Williams thought it was quite clear that Rhodes was the unscrupulous leader of a gold-seeking gang and had deceived his Queen, his country, and his shareholders (1899, 54-5).

Few contemporary politicians were regarded with respect. Perhaps the most disliked was A. J. Balfour whose share in the Education Act of 1902 aroused great hostility in Wales. Rev. A. Wynne Thomas, M.A., Aberystwyth, said the storm of opposition would rage and would bring to an end Balfour's career, not as a golfer but as a statesman (1904, 51). There were frequent yearnings for a man of the calibre of Gladstone or Bright, though it is easy to venerate the dead who have gone beyond the arena where decisions on controversial affairs have to be made. It is probable that neither of these leaders would in 1902 have made decisions which would have commended them to Welsh nonconformists. Rev. J. D. Evans, M.A., Liverpool, said that there was only one politician whom he respected though he differed from almost all his opinions, and that was Lord Hugh Cecil, who "is a man who dares to appeal to conscience".

Among the numerous Welsh politicians only one emerged into great fame beyond the Principality. There were occasional references to the expanding prestige of Lloyd George. He was once described as the most popular man in Wales; this fame was gained in the first instance by his championship of the burial rights of non-conformists. Mr. Augustus Lewis referred in 1904 to Lloyd George who "has behind him the sacred conviction of a nation that their religious liberties are being unfairly and unjustifiably attacked" (1904, 51). In 1909 Rev. J. Glyn Davies visualised a Church where the millionaire and the pauper would both be reckoned as men and he saw a foretaste of this in a recent incident where an aged saint of seventy had received the Sacrament alongside Lloyd George who was by then the Chancellor of the Exchequer and who had just secured the Old Age Pension for the old man with whom he received the Sacrament (1909, 24).

Britain's power had been unchallenged for so long that it had come to be accepted without question and few discerned any signs of the approaching storm of the First World War. As early as 1895 Rev. R. Hughes, M.A., Aberystwyth, had spoken in general terms of war as directly opposed to Christ's teaching (1895, 97). In 1909 Sir J. H. Roberts spoke of the increasing burden of armaments which was a strange phenomenon after 2,000 years of the so-called reign of the Prince of Peace (1909, 63). Mr. W. Brace, M.P., called for arbitration and conciliation as a means of solving disputes and said that the diplomats who caused wars should be made to wage them and not the thousands who have no quarrel with each other (1909, 69). In 1911,

Rev. E. G. Miles, Liverpool, thought there was a growing awareness of the wrongs inflicted by war ; hitherto there had been no "concern for the misery wars entailed". Britain was spending sixty millions annually upon armaments and this was more than could or ought to be afforded ; other nations were also spending far too much. Miles held there was an increasing demand for Christian modes of settling disputes, and the Red Cross was an attempt to ameliorate the wounds of war. He was sure that the Churches together could further transmit this spirit (1911, 56-8). Rev. J. Talog Davies, Cardiff, supported this plea and said that even as things were it was the Gospel which had prevented the world from sinking in "a welter of a blood-thirsty barbarism". He referred to a recent statement by George Bernard Shaw that Christianity was a failure but the Church need not be alarmed "for George Bernard Shaw has to say something startling on an average once a week or his friends will think he is dead or ill". Davies admitted that the Church's history contained bleak pages and that there were those outside the organised Christianity who had a greater hatred of war and of social and moral evils than those inside (1911, 59-63).

In 1912 Rev. T. G. Owen, the retiring President, also hoped that the spirit of peace was increasing but he had misgivings in view of the continuing expenditure on armaments and also because of the aggressive and foolish policy of Britain in the South African War when she was prepared to lose 25,000 lives and £250 millions even though nine-tenths of her demands had been conceded by the Boers (1912, 32).

Just as there had been no adulation of war prior to 1914 the years after the Great War brought further disillusion. In 1919 the retiring President, Mr. John Owens, J.P., said that war and its sufferings had not led to a greater sense of brotherhood in the community nor to an appreciation of the higher things of life. He echoed a recent remark by Lloyd George in the City Temple wherein he wondered why the unselfishness, comradeship and valour shown in war had not survived into the time of peace. Owens also attacked the Press campaign to vilify Lloyd George which ranged from the cynicism of the *Times* to the vulgar abuse of the *Daily News*. Owens, however, did profess to discern signs of revival and thought that any church which felt the need of revival would get it (1919, 12).

The Rt. Hon. J. Herbert Lewis, M.P., spoke in 1919 of the state of the Church after the War and said that while soldiers returning to rural areas had taken their place again in the churches there were other areas where threequarters of the soldiers declined to rejoin and he thought they were not to blame, for after the sacrifices of Flanders they were tired of the trivialities which filled so much church life and especially with the denominational differences which had torn Wales. The Church needed to take a wide interest in all aspects of life. For example, it ought to follow up the raising of the school-leaving age to fourteen by insisting on the provision of further educational opportunities up to at least eighteen (1919, 25-7). Mr. J. Mortimer Harris, Hoylake, said there was need for a drastic self-examination by the Church. Organised Churches had perished in the past because they failed to welcome opportunities and lost their enthusiasm, enterprise, and loyalty. Many Christians lived on the level of minimal obedience and so it was little wonder outsiders thought they could live an even higher life without any link to the Church. The Church had often shown a narrow and conservative spirit and, unlike businessmen and politicians, had stuck "in the old ruts" and had withdrawn from many fields of life. The Church in his view, had been too silent on social and industrial questions and on the temperance issue. Harris also thought the Church should show its attitude to the League of Nations. Unless the Church took an interest in such questions it could not hope to convince or convert the people (1919, 22-3). It is easy to demand changes but less easy to suggest specific changes which can win general assent within a church. Rev. Richard Jones, Llandinam, also demanded that the Church should face up to the opportunity offered by the peace and he was convinced that "men who can speak about God and duty, Christ and salvation, with knowledge and in no uncertain tones, will not fail of a hearing". The war had broken up conventional civilisation and defective Christian witness. War had revealed to him, as to all chaplains, the astonishing ignorance which abounded concerning the rudiments of the Christian faith and life ; there was an urgent need for an appeal to the intelligence as well as to the emotions. There was also an urgent need to measure current industrial practices by Christian standards so as to break the long reign of economic systems which devalued human beings. Jones held there was a growing oneness of the world and an inescapable responsibility of people for one another. Christians had a commission to the whole world but any approach to Africa, for example, had to be made in penitence for past injustices inflicted upon that land. "The hour calls not for despairing men and women but for those who have the courage to believe greatly in the power of God" (1919, 27-33).

In 1920 the retiring President, Rev. William Mendus, spoke of the spirit of revolution in the world ; for example, in Ireland, "terror reigns in that unhappy island". At home, there was class-hatred, distrust, pleasure-seeking, money-grabbing, gambling, drunkenness, immorality, suicides, murders, and other crimes. The Church was not what it ought to be. There were those who saw elements of "rubbish" in the Confession of Faith and even in the Bible but there was certainly "rubbish" in the pulpit, in the Big Seat, and in the pews generally. There was need of fresh discipline and he thought much was to be gained from the breakdown of prejudices and barriers between Churches (1920, 9-13).

In 1920 Major W. P. Wheldon, M.A., D.S.O., who was later to receive a knighthood for his services to Wales and to education, gave a far-ranging address on world problems. He admitted that even by 1920 the "cloud-capped towers of the League of Nations are fading out of sight" though its achievement ought not to be minimised. He then referred to three perennial problems, namely, reconciliation with enemies, co-existence with allies, and concern for backward nations. Wheldon said that the feeling against the U.S.A. and France was almost more acute than that against Germany. He ascribed this to the fact that success in war depends on being "prepared to tell very big lies about it the whole time". Normally "you go to the House of Lords for them as a rule", but in war lies were told on both sides on a vast scale ; when told about enemies little damage was done since both sides knew they were lies, but when indulged in between allies the inevitable disillusion after hostilities was shattering. In war the allies praised each others efforts but after the struggle each nation wished to claim the credit for itself and so to belittle its allies, and "the Russians we do not pretend even to reconcile". Wheldon paid tribute to Lloyd George as the only man ready to make a reconciling step towards the Russians but "Churchill has been too many for him in that direction". He said that in facing current problems both justice and generosity would be needed. Provided there was no recrudescence of the martial spirit in Germany he was not without hope of better relations with Germany. Generosity meant sacrifice but without it he did not see how the problems of India, Egypt, Mesopotamia and Ireland could be solved. He admitted a solution to the Irish problem was not yet in sight ; strength and weakness had been tried alternately for eight hundred years ; a further Civil War would not solve the problem ; "you cannot kill the people" ; however, unless it was solved, "if this mischief continues, it will tear the British Empire to pieces" (1920, 37-40). Rev. Thomas Yates was no more encouraging in 1923 when he said that Europe was still sullenly and stubbornly unwilling for any deep-going revision of its ancient procedures but was obsessed with the idea of war's inevitability (1923, 38). Many of these points were taken up by Rev. J. H. Howard, M.A., Colwyn Bay, in 1924. He referred to the innate conservatism of the human race. Reformers were sent to the Cross and saints were rarely welcomed ; though venerated after their death they would not be welcome if they returned. Change was inescapable because just as people outgrew their clothes so they outgrew creeds, dogmas, programmes and parties. Nature opened the door to change by removing leaders who had outlived their service and their vision. Even the restlessness and social feverishness in Britain were better than death, and "never was the world so interesting a place to live in". War had caused unrest and disillusion but there had also been an awakening to inequalities, particularly in the values given to people and things ; men had been conscripted but money had been borrowed at 5% interest. Leaders, whether politicians or parsons, had been discredited by their mismanagement of world affairs so as to lead to the tragedy of war. Old parochial and national and imperial frontiers were discarded ideals ignored by finance, science and commerce. It was difficult for those over forty to appreciate the changes but it was useless to pretend they did not exist. Howard saw hope in such movements as C.O.P.E.C. and the S.V.M.U., and for all the faults of the Church there was no other place where distinctions disappeared so much. Nevertheless, there was an atheism among Christians which had not yet grasped the contradiction between the Gospel spirit and war. For the first two centuries the Church had been opposed to war and had been accused of undermining the Empire but the attitude gradually changed to toleration of war, and then under Constantine's patronage to the encouragement of imperial campaigns. There had always been dissident groups such as Donatists, Cathari and Anabaptists, but their doctrinal eccentricities were sufficient to stifle their protests against war. However, the time had again arrived for the Church to make war on war, including class and industrial warfare (1924, 46-9).

A strong attack upon current attitudes was made by Rev. George M. Llewelyn Davies in 1926. He had become a pacifist in the War and had been imprisoned for his activities; he later became the Member of Parliament for the University of Wales and had been deeply involved in public affairs.[1] In the "wild world of politics" he said there was little real desire for peace. A thousand would attend a military tattoo for every ten who would go to a peace meeting. There had been talk of repentance during the War but the nation did not repent of what it was doing, and when the War was over talk about repentance was smothered by talk about "terrible justice", and, in his opinion, this was the cause of the disputes and industrial depression. He quoted Mr. Reginald McKenna, a former Chancellor of the Exchequer, for the view that the demand for reparations would prove to be a curse, and he made the disputable assertion that forgiveness was not only good Christianity but good business. He also said that the Church had not shown the world a better way; indeed the Church had lost its own way and had discredited its own message by its failure to reconcile its own antagonised sects. He told of a recent conference in Bavaria attended by two hundred and fifty people of every colour, creed and caste, Roman Catholics, Lutherans, aristocrats and workers, and where the fun and friendliness had been a stark contrast to "our cold and bored and narrow little church meetings in Wales" (1926, 64-71). It can be remarked that the experience of conferences in congenial surroundings without enduring or close commitments is likely to be much different from that which develops where a wide diversity of persons has to live together from week to week.

Rev. Morgan Watcyn Williams, M.C., spoke in 1927 of the bitterness and "poison which flows in the anaemic veins of Europe", and also festered in the body politic at home. He said that the trouble with the nation and the world was tardiness to forgive and until this was done man's heroic instincts would be expended on war which was a waste of heroism. He said there was a clear call to the heroism of Christ who could trust the publican, love the unlovely, and criticise the wealthy, "the last people in the world we are courageous with" (1927, 40-4).

In his valedictory address in 1928, the President, Rev. D. M. Rees, Tredegar, said the time was one of unrest and opportunity. The great growth of groups and corporations "belittles man and makes life cheap". The Church had to stress the value of the individual and the need of a right relationship with God and his fellowmen, but the Church was crippled by worldliness, speed and spite. Rees said that the Church had become an aggregation of noisy activities and was often like a literary or amusement society, a social club or a business venture.

Rev. J. Morgan Jones, M.A., Merthyr, contrasted the current outlook with that prevailing in his childhood ; the social structure, including the extremes of wealth and poverty, was accepted as a fixed foundation but there had arisen a wave of change which put all institutions into a flux, and he forecast that triumphant science would destroy its own achievement (1928, 50). Jones became President in 1929 and in his valedictory address in 1930 he reverted to the extent and rapidity of change. Industrial processes were causing a revolution without the usual throes of revolution. All institutions and conventions were being questioned and old pieties were being eroded. The virtues of wonder, reverence, and modesty were being dismissed as old-fashioned, "Victorian, I think, is the word". The Church had to live in this changing atmosphere. A new culture, self-sufficient, self-reliant, unrestrained, unethical, and irreligious, was arising. Young ministers were going into "a conflict far more bitter than any that I and my contemporaries have ever endured". He said the Church itself was ill-fitted to face the future and he did not know which of the attitudes labelled as Fundamentalist or Modernist was the more perverse (1930, 18-20).

Mr. W. H. Williams, B.L., Newport, gave a sombre sketch of the world situation in 1930. He said there was much talk about peace but "man's actions are in the other direction towards war preparations, and in Italy, Russia, Germany, France, and England, pledges to renounce war were fading into history, and pacts would only be observed as long as it is expedient that they should be observed". In such a frame of mind war would be inevitable unless injustices were removed and unless there was a change of heart. There was great inequality in the distribution of the world's resources, and hungry nations were the "objects of a legalised system of unscrupulous robbery on exchange". Unemployment was a topic of party recrimination but little was done to ease the plight of the victims. The Church had a duty to rebuke and guide. It would be criticised on the ground that it was trespassing beyond its proper sphere but the Church had a duty and could influence events. His estimate of the Church's influence was perhaps too favourable as was his view that it was the Church which had rallied the nation in the Great War ; without the Church's influence, "all hope of success would have been adandoned in a few weeks" (1930, 73-80).

In 1931, the retiring President, Rev. John Edwards, Wrexham, said that the Church had always had to face difficulties but this was a pre-condition of its progress. Restlessness among youth was not new and he quoted from an ancient Byzantine manuscript ; "Alas, times are not what they used to be ; children no longer obey their parents, and everyman wants to write a book" (1931, 19).

In the nineteen-thirties there were references to the rise of the dictators. In 1933 Rev. J. Henry Davies spoke of Mussolini gloating over the crushing of liberty (1933, 59). Mr. Rhys Davies, M.P., was surely making the understatement of the conferences when he said that at best current political trends were doubtfully in line with the teaching of Jesus. He thought it was hypocritical for nations to pretend to support the League of Nations and at the same time maintain armament firms and a military caste. The destruction of food in order to maintain prices, the suppression of freedom in Italy, Yugoslavia, and other countries, the terms of the Treaty of Versailles and of the Ottawa agreements for imperial preference, the contiguity of luxury and poverty, and the continuing enmity of France and Germany were sinister factors. Davies then made the first conference reference to Hitler and the brutalities poured by his regime upon the Jews. He saw war clouds gathering and he listed as contributory factors the lust for power and conquest, the commercial exploitation, the profits from armaments, the narrow nationalisms, the pressure of populations, the tension of opposing creeds, and racial animosity and fears (1933, 74-7). In 1934 Rev. D. O. Calvin Thomas, M.A., recalled that he had started his ministry soon after 1918, and in the succeeding years "the evil fruits of the ghastly crime of that war have been becoming ever and increasingly ripe for the plucking" ; however, he believed there were signs of fresh breezes (1934, 73-7). However, such breezes as there were were soon to be swallowed up in the storm of another war Speaking in the same conference, Rev. Howell Williams, Cardiff, said there was an air of bankruptcy in many spheres and there was no vision in the realms of commerce, industry, statesmanship, and ecclesiastical life. Leaders were ready to follow any will-o-the-wisp. Most leaders in civic, educational, and commercial circles were church members and yet seemed stagnant, impotent and nervy (1934, 27-33). Rev. John Roberts also spoke of the evaporation of the Liberal Party and said that the Connexion which had once been so closely linked to that party was now sharing in its twilight (1934, 46-51).

In 1935, the Mayor of Colwyn Bay told the Conference that the suspicion and discontent in the world were driving the people to dictators and wars (1935, 5). Prof. Levi also spoke of the threat of war but gave a somewhat ambiguous statement of the Christian attitude. He said that the safety of the state might demand a recourse to arms but this ought to be no concern of the members of the Church; they must ignore war and have no part in it. He did not indicate how a Christian could opt out of membership of a state or how a policy could be right for a state which was wrong for the Christian (1935, 46). The normal pacifist attitude is that war is wrong for both individuals and the state. Rev. E. L. Mendus diagnosed pleasure-seeking and Sabbath-breaking as symptoms of the surging tide of materialism in the world. Moreover, humanism had permeated current thought and man had been made the measure of all things. This could lead to a disillusionment which would be the beginning of the cry for God but Mendus thought a divided Church was in no position to lead. Rev. D. S. Owen, who was to exercise a great ministry at Jewin Chapel in London, said that humanity had lost its nerve and he quoted Dean Matthews for the view that the majority of civilised people believed that in this world only was there any hope and that even if God existed he was irrelevant to human calculations. Little wonder, said Owen, that depression had seized the heart of man. Man had claimed self-sufficiency but the result had been a loss of individual status and freedom. Men were afraid of themselves and of one another, and this was all the more terrifying now that science had united the world and brought distant lands together. Nevertheless, if the time was one of crisis, it was also a time of opportunity and challenge (1935, 56-62).

Rev. Howell Williams, B.A., Hoylake, said that a proud independent world was on the brink of suicide. He held that the contemporary upsurge of dictatorship was a diseased mutation of theocracy. Democracy had been abandoned because people were not fit for its responsibilities, and Williams regarded this as a sign that at heart every political and scientific problem was a moral problem (1935, 23-7).

In 1936 Rev. F. W. Cole, Cardiff devoted his valedictory address as President to a grim survey of the world's predicament. Democracy and freedom were in peril and nations were bewildered. Nations professed to seek peace but made poison gas. Nations were members of the League of Nations yet each nation was preparing for war. In Great Britain there were almost two million unemployed. Individually, ethical standards were in a state of change and temptations seemed to be irresistible (1936, 11-2).

This theme was continued by Rev. Richard Jones, Llandinam, who by 1937 had gained the rare honour of a Doctorate of Divinity from Queen's University, Belfast. In his presidential address he spoke of the persecutions being endured by Orthodox, Roman Catholic and Protestant Churches. The Church was ill-fitted to face the attack because of its divisions based on nationality, creed and organisation but he believed that the Oxford Conference on Life and Work which he had just attended was a symptom of an attempt by the Churches to face up to their duty in the dangerous world situation. He had learned at the Conference that whereas nations had to begin their negotiations from a position of division Churches began from the fact of an already existing and indestructible unity (1937, 16-8). Mr. Dudley Howe, J.P., Barry, then surveyed the insecurity, suspicion, and fear which filled the world. The international scene was strewn with scraps of paper. He saw the struggle in Europe as one between Christian civilisation and a blind barbarism whose victory would lead to the worst of deaths, the death of freedom. War was, however, the outcome of deep causes which would have to be eliminated before the threat of war would abate. Many who professed to support the League of Nations wished also to retain their own comforts undisturbed, but the eradication of the causes of war would involve sacrifice. A first and immediate step was the establishment of an international police force because without this France could not be expected to feel any sense of security (1937, 35-41).

Rev. George M. Ll. Davies, whose radical views have been noted already, said that war was never unpopular in England and was not an occasional phenomena. Even in peacetime gangster exploits attracted more interest than did patient heroisms. There was no general will to justice and equity, and there had been no repentance of war or of the violence and inequality of peacetime. Economic oppressions and suppressions bred war, and if people prepared for war they would get war. Power might secure a pause but it could not produce peace. Davies said that power had not pacified Ireland nor secured prohibition in the U.S.A., and he said that from his experience of having lived for two years in four prisons he had learned that power could neither change man nor save society. Having satisfied himself that there could be no legitimate use of power he announced that he could no longer support the League of Nations Union since it was associated with the policy of military sanctions to ensure collective security. He praised George Lansbury for resigning from the leadership of the Labour Party rather than be associated with the rearmament campaign. He laid the blame for the rise of Nazism in Germany upon the policy pursued by Britain and others whereby one and a half million Germans had been allowed to starve. Germany had also been cut off from raw materials and had been denied colonies for her crowded population. Davies assailed the ecclesiastical policy which had sanctified war. The Cardinal Archbishop of Milan had blessed Italian troops. Lutheran pastors had been supporters of the German war effort. Archbishop Lang of Canterbury had reaffirmed the position of the Thirty-nine Articles that the sword may be the minister of God for the protection of the weak, but he ignored the fact that whatever truth the Article had in the past the sword now meant explosions, bombs, and gas. The Archbishop of Wales had told cadets at a bombing school at Lleyn that there was no inconsistency between their profession and that of a Christian. Archbishop William Temple was also quoted as saying that pacifism was a heresy. Archbishops and Bishops reflected the conventional climate which was shared by most people. Davies told the Conference that Dick Shepherd had told him that when he spoke on peace at the Church Assembly he felt "as welcome as a temperance orator at a policeman's picnic". In his view the defection of the Church from its true function was shown by the fine statement of the recent Oxford Conference that war was a distortion of truth and a display of the power of sin. Many were ready to depend upon the powers of this world. Davies challenged the Church to depend upon the power of a peace-making which stood disarmed (1937, 42-52).

The shadow of war was very close in 1938. A telegram was sent to Mr. Neville Chamberlain, the Prime Minister, hoping that war would be averted (1938, 43). Rev. M. Watcyn Williams, B.A., M.C., said that politics without religion was a doomed enterprise but also a religion which shirked its political and social obligations was not Christian. However, he was under no illusions as to the difficulty of tracing the hand of God in history. If it was claimed that God was on the side of the allies in the Great War, it was hard to see why He should have allowed the weather which ruined Haig's plans at Passchendale. If it was God's will to abolish the slave-trade, it was hard to account for the wage slavery under which many people had still to live. Moreover, there were those who confidently attributed the Great War to God who wished to penalise the nation for its intemperance or for the disestablishment of the Church in Wales. Again, the Christian claim that God was at work in history was challenged by many other and often mutually incompatible interpretations. Some saw history as a series of cycles; others saw it as an inevitable progress, often to an undefined goal; others interpreted the historical process on a materialist or on a totalitarian basis. Williams thought that enough account had not been taken of the dynamic movement of history and he thought that the Greek influence, by stressing the impassibility of God and thereby ruling out patripassianism, had made it difficult to think of God as active in history. Hebrew thought was concentrated much more on the mighty acts of God, and Williams said that the Christian doctrine of the incarnation meant that God plunged into history. Williams must have been one of the earliest readers of Tillich whom he quoted as saying that "truth dwells in the midst of struggle and fate, not in an immobile beyond". This stress on the movement of God in history was not an equating of the Kingdom of God with any earthly Utopia. The Kingdom of God was a judgement on any given society, capitalist, nationalist, or dictatorial. These types of society were committed to international economic and ideological war, and all who took the sword would perish by the sword. Williams thought the Church was blinded by its bourgeois connections and concentrated its hopes for revival upon individual piety or mass hysteria which fostered a piety which used God to maintain the status quo. The Church also professed to rebuke the materialism of the unemployed who protested against their conditions of life but the Church was at the same time concerned about the Central Fund and Pensions for ministers. However, God would not be exploited (1938, 28-35).

Dr. Richard Jones saw many of his hopes disappearing in the world-wide trend to dictatorship. The omnicompetent state was spreading its tentacles and another war would hasten this trend. He regarded war as essentially evil and stupid and an outrage against humanity. He claimed that absolute pacifism was the only consistent position; he admitted that many Christians did not share this view but he held they ought not to regard pacifists as wild idealists. Even such a recognition of the pacifist position would fall short of a reconciliation in Christ, and Dr. Jones said he agreed with Dr. C. E. Raven that a further war would probably lead to a pacifist secession from the Church and thus further mutilate the already divided Body of Christ (1938, 44-8).

Chapter VII

THE CHURCH AND ITS YOUNG PEOPLE

EVERY branch of the Church is always concerned to secure the loyalty of its young people. Unless they can be instructed in the Faith and given reasonable grounds for accepting it no denomination is likely to survive. Effective continuity also requires that they should be won to take their place as full members of the Church. This has always been a formidable task since a genuine faith cannot be imposed by force ; excessive indoctrination often causes revulsion, and there are also periods when the climate of opinion favours the rejection of what is traditional.

Presbyterians in Wales had to face a number of local difficulties. The system of education provided in State schools did not include religious instruction. In 1870 non-conformists had fought for its exclusion so as to prevent their children from being indoctrinated by Anglican teachers. However, it was not long before some ministers were questioning the wisdom of this policy. Many children never attended any Sunday school and this meant that they got no religious education in any school. Rev. J. Douglas Watters asked in 1893 if it was still necessary for the Free Churches to stand for the same policy ; he thought their duty as Christian citizens ought to give them a wider vision than denominational advantages and he thought it might be possible for Biblical knowledge to be taught in the State schools (1893, 18). In 1899 Rev. John Hughes, Holyhead, wondered if there was no way out of the dilemma of choosing between no religious instruction at all and the giving of sectarian teaching disguised as religious instruction. He was sure that there was the common ground of Scripture which could be taught but he thought that the Established Church had taken advantage of its privileged position to win over many young people by means of daily indoctrination (1899, 49). It was this fear which made co-operation in this field very difficult ; the 1904 Education Act had exacerbated the antipathy and government support for Anglican schools in rural areas was regarded as a deliberate attempt to undermine non-conformity. In these circumstances the Church had to depend for the propagation of its teaching upon the Sunday schools and by 1900 there was considerable uneasiness about the efficiency with which these schools were carried on. Thus the Connexion had to face the problem of what had to be taught and how it was to be taught.

There was general recognition that religion could not be implanted by force. At the first Conference in 1889 Mr. E. J. Baillie, F.L.S., Chester, spoke of what he called the three R's in the training of the young ; the first was reverence which included reverence for God, for holy things, and for parents, and he frowned upon references to a father as "the governor" or "the old man" ; there was also need for resolution and rectitude (1889, 21). Puleston Jones followed with a plea for a proper balance of discipline and love in training the young ; he said this was no new problem and quoted a comment dating from the time of Anselm that children could not be kept in order. Jones saw a special threat to the young in the newspapers ; "Keep the young as much as you can from newspapers" (1894, 24). In 1895 Rev. Maurice Griffiths, Llanidloes, said the only effective means to win the young were love, discipline and spirituality, in that order. There was need of discipline to correct the faults of youth, for youth had faults, but to begin there was to fail. It was in his view the mark of an age of Pharisaism to associate virtue with grey hairs, and he saw little point in the tirades against youth which were often heard in sermons (1895, 87-8). Mrs. John Pugh thought that there had been an undue reaction against the extreme discipline of bygone times, but "storming at the faults of children may terrify them ; it does not lead them to leave them" ; there was need of the drawing power of almighty love (1897, 49). In 1898 the retiring President, Mr. William Evans, J.P., Southport, said that the young people would not be held by the severe regime of the past but by a loving and generous sympathy (1898, 27). In 1903 Rev. E. Rowland, Crickhowell, said it was necessary to offer sympathy and friendliness to the young and without that it would be impossible to gain their attachment and co-operation ; he held that the "crude opinions of youth" were not to be met with alarm but ought to be regarded as evidence of expanding thought and ought not to be judged severely or harshly suppressed since it was better to think, even sceptically, than never to think at all (1903, 44).

However, in spite of high ideals, there was an alarming decline in the number of Sunday school scholars. Rev. J. Douglas Watters said that his own researches confirmed a recent finding that nine out of every ten Sunday school scholars eventually lost touch with the

Church, and he estimated that 45,000 scholars in British Sunday schools annually drifted into intemperance; he also stated that in Leeds jail 230 prisoners out of 282 had once been Sunday school scholars (1893, 17). The decline continued on into the next century. In 1925 Mr. Derry Evans, M.A., said that two-thirds of Britain's Sunday school scholars drifted from all church connection between the ages of fourteen and eighteen. He said that in 1914 there had been 27,538 teachers and 182,088 scholars in the Connexional schools, a total of 209,626; in 1924 there were 24,382 teachers and 161,836 scholars, a total of 186,218 and a decrease of 23,408. These figures are not easily reconciled with those of Mr. Owens whose figure for scholars in 1918 was 190,825 which was more than Evans gave for 1914; if Owens figures include teachers the decline was even more rapid than Evans estimated. However both were convinced of the fact of decline. Evans said this was due in part to the ravages of the War, the decline in the birth-rate, and the attractions of modern life. The Bible, according to Evans, was a closed book and had been replaced by literature of low taste and morals; family worship had ceased (1925, 49-51). Rev. John Edwards, Wrexham, admitted in his valedictory address as President in 1931 that Sunday school membership was decreasing but nothing better had been devised to replace it (1931, 21).

It was also felt by some speakers that the spread of higher education had weakened the Sunday schools. Mr. Henry Lewis, J.P., said that the growing University of Wales took young people from their homes at an early age and disturbed old patterns of life. One hundred and fifty were gaining degrees yearly at the University of Wales and a large proportion of them then left the country (1908, 46). Mr. E. Madoc Jones, M.A., Beaumaris, pointed out that many who had been educated in schools and colleges were "idlers in the Lord's Vineyard". However, in his view, this was a challenge to the Church to raise the quality of its teaching because young people would no longer be won or held by ecclesiastical cant or unnatural restraint (1908, 44-5). In 1920 Rev. R. J. Rees referred to the expanding extra-mural studies organised by the University which had appointed organisers for South Wales and West Wales. Men of ability were also being sent to Ruskin College, Oxford, to be trained so as to "teach the youths of the valleys certain phases of industry". Compared with this Rees said that Sunday school expansion was slight and mainly in English speaking churches, and the increase of 400 in the preceding year had come after twenty years of decline. The intake during the period of the Revival had not balanced the overall leakage and "we are not having the pick of our youth in our Sunday Schools" ; this was bound to lead to a shortage of satisfactory teachers in the future (1920, 45-50). In 1926, Rev. George M. Llewelyn Davies, always a stormy petrel on the Welsh scene, said that modern education laid far too much emphasis upon success and discipline. He thought that far too many were ready to take Solomon's advice ; "Spare the rod and spoil the child" ; but "Solomon knew little of the heart of a child or of a woman or he would never have thought he could marry a thousand of them". It was, in his view, Jesus and not Solomon who understood the deep things of children and woman. Davies paid tribute to the work of Baroness Montessori who had taught that the genius of the child required freedom, friendliness and co-operation rather than discipline, and he said that her work would be remembered when "Mussolini and his antics are consigned to the darkness they deserve". This was the first reference to the Italian dictator and was more perceptive of Mussolini's worth than was common in the twenties. Davies held that the educational method tended to make children into idolaters of the world's standards of success and there was little point in bemoaning the competitive spirit in the world when it was impressed upon the young in schools (1926, 68-70).

It was against this background of educational theory and of widening educational opportunity that Sunday schools had to carry on their work.

All speakers were convinced that the content of the message to be proclaimed was to be found in the Bible but recent changes in Biblical study had forced them to advocate a discriminating use of the Bible. Principal John Hughes, the Normal College, Bangor, stressed the unity of all knowledge, and religion was, in his view, a habit of mind essential for the study of all subjects, and the aim should be to lead the young to believe what was true, to sympathise with what was noble, and to know and do what was right. The young had to be given a standard of judgement so as to make a wise use of the Bible and he repented that he had once set a class of boys to learn parts of Leviticus ; that had been "a wicked waste of time" (1896, 66-8). He also laid down principles which applied to all fields of learning ; the lesson had to be adapted to the pupil's capacity, had also to be clearly arranged and appropriately illustrated and, above all, had to be interesting.

Rev. W. Glynne, Manchester, spoke of the spiritual indigestion caused by futile cramming (1896, 71). Mrs. Walter Lloyd, Aberdare, a lady of Scottish birth, thought there was "no more effective means of instruction than a good catechism well-taught". Rev. John Williams, Cardiff, commended the *Christian Instructor* or the *Shorter Catechism* as valuable methods of instruction in the Faith. Rev. John Owen, Tonypandy, brought a salutary warning to the Conference when he said that the natural perversity in children was such that religious instruction went against the grain and he thought there was need for teaching the Bible in such a way as to centre upon the greatness and goodness of God ; the harvest could not be guaranteed (1896, 72-3).

There were many criticisms of the methods used in Sunday schools. In 1899 Rev. Richard Jones thought it was high time to readjust their methods to make them more effective and this was also stressed by Rev. John Hughes, Holyhead (1899, 49). Alderman Jones Griffiths said it was still often assumed that it was the task of the Sunday schools to teach people to read but this was a waste of time since it was better done by trained teachers in day schools. Also, in his view, much time was wasted in cramming the Sunday school pupils with scriptural facts and figures, even with genealogies. He also thought it was unfair to subject children to theological disquisitions. The syllabus prescribed for Connexional examinations also seemed to him to encourage a wasteful use of time. The aim should be to teach the great truths and principles of the Faith and should offer training in worship suited to the children's capacity. He even suggested children's services to be held concurrently with adult services. Some teachers were ready to use a blackboard to illustrate their theme and even to use a magic-lantern on Sunday evenings, notwithstanding "ominous shakes of the head from certain good old brethren" (1899, 45-6).

Prof. W. Jenkin Jones, M.A., Aberystwyth, said that teachers must have something to teach and must teach in a form within the child's capacity. He advised teachers to begin with the Gospels so that the Old Testament might be read in the light of the New and measured by its standard. He held there was a place for memorisation but the material memorised should not be too far ahead of understanding. He held that the memorising of historical passages, however Biblical, was "the last refuge of stupidity", and he also feared that the stress upon examinations was a "lamentable conversion to the spirit of the world" whereby ability rather than goodness gained the rewards

(1901, 36-8). Mr. E. W. Jones, M.A., the County School, Barry, thought that the exclusion of religious instruction from the state schools laid a heavy responsibility upon the Sunday schools to use effective methods and keep in step with educational advance. He said there was need for separate classrooms as this would improve both discipline and the quality of teaching. He thought that the Sunday school activities should cover the physical, literary and musical fields. "It is time we in Wales should burst the bonds of convention that fetter us". He also put forward plans for the more adequate training of teachers. He thought that the Infant Department should make imaginative and ethical use of the Bible stories, and the message could be illustrated by pictures, songs and stories from many lands, and a magic lantern could be used though "probably prejudice is too strong against such a disregard of convention". In the Junior Department the Life of Christ ought to be the central theme of study, while among Seniors the Epistles of Paul and the Gospel of John would supply deeper material, and at this stage he advised a paragraph rather than a verse as the unit of study (1901, 41-3). Mr. T. C. Thomas, Bedlinog, supported much of this and said that educational advance had shown up the poverty of much of their Sunday school work; the methods were often antiquated, the quality of the teaching was often dry and barren, and there was also "an appalling indifference upon the part of parents" (1901, 44). Rev. W. Lewis, Pontypridd, suggested the appointment of a lady superintendent now and again; while not condemning all preparation for examinations he thought there was a danger that cramming could take precedence over heart and conscience (1901, 47). Miss Tydvil Evans held that memorisation was not a test of progress and in fact encouraged the development of wrong motives in the young. She then made what she admitted was an unorthodox assertion when she said that there was "a great deal of rubbish about teaching very little children the catechism" (1901, 47). Rev. D. T. Evans was moved to declare that there were "great advantages in preparing for examinations" (1901, 48).

Mr. H. H. Meyler, M.A., Machynlleth, said that the quality of the teachers was more important than the quality of the teaching. He feared that many who professed to lead the young had become old before their time and had ceased to inspire, influence, sympathise with, or understand those whom they taught (1904, 82). Mr. Horsfall Turner, B.A., Llanidloes, also emphasised the need for a sympathetic understanding of the young. A teacher could not make any impact if he expected the young to live as he lived in his own youth or if he thought he could convince by laying down bare assertions of orthodox teaching. A teacher had to put himself in the position of the young who were facing difficulties he never knew ; it was, for example, not sufficient to condemn certain types of literature without giving reasons why these should be avoided (1905, 80-1).

Many speakers, such as Rev. R. J. Rees, reiterated the need for modern educational methods and for the provision of suitable literature for teachers (1920, 50), but there was little agreement on the nature of the changes required. Some advocated Pleasant Sunday Afternoons, Brotherhoods and Sacred Concerts, but Alderman S. N. Jones, the retiring President spoke in 1911 about the injury which such activities did to the Church by obscuring the important work of teaching the Word of God and Gospel hymns (1911, 33). The problem of holding the young in the Sunday schools became even more complex as the years went by and some were even tempted to rail even more at the waywardness of youth. In their defence, Rev. J. H. Davies, Ewloe Green, said in his retiring presidential address in 1929 that young people were often unfairly judged. They were criticised for their dress and extravagance : "How prone to judge youth by the clothes it wears !" However, in his view, drunkenness among youth was now exceptional whereas a generation earlier it was regarded as a sign of manliness. Youth were being exploited by middle-aged men. The young had been brought up in difficult times but they were not afraid of life and adventure. He also directed attention to the place of the young in the work of the Church ; this was more creditable than was often allowed, and if there were fewer young people in the churches there were also less of the old, not to mention the serious defaulters among those in middle-life (1929, 20-1).

In addition to the Sunday school there were other organisations which were open to the young and which were referred to by various speakers. In 1895 Rev. Maurice Griffiths, Llanidloes, commended the recently founded Christian Endeavour movement as a fruitful means of Christian nurture (1895, 87-9). In 1899 Rev. Richard Jones also commended the movement but with reservations ; he thought there might be a danger of encouraging a narrow individualism rather than fostering a hallowing of the whole of life, and he felt that "much wicked mischief is done by encouraging very young people to proclaim their own religious experiences" and he thought that some of the movement's forms of censorship were scarcely calculated to win the sympathies of the more intelligent young people (1899, 41). Jones then went on to suggest the founding of a distinctive denominational Young People's Guild (1899, 42). In the next yearly Conference a plan for the establishment of such a Guild was introduced. It proposed the setting up of a central Guild to co-ordinate the work among the young in the whole Connexion and to bring the needs of the young before the Courts of the Church and to foster a sense of unity and fellowship among the young. It was suggested that one of the Conference meetings should be devoted to the young and this started a tradition which is continued in the Association in the East. Branch Guilds were envisaged in every local church (1900, 16). These suggestions did not attain practical fulfilment, and most churches, particularly the smaller ones, continued to work mainly through the Sunday schools. Social and educational changes as well as theological variations within the Church were unfavourable to the growth of such a movement. Even in the years since the Second World War the lively Young People's Fellowship has evoked interest in only a minority of the English-speaking churches.

In 1905 much praise was given to the work of organisations such as the Boys' Brigade which had twenty companies in Newport (1905, 84-6). There were also those who thought that local groups specially designed to meet local needs and without external links would be very useful. Rev. F. W. Cole said that the Revival had gripped many young people and swept them along into changed living and worthy service of others. He urged the churches to make room for enthusiasm; Jesus had been so enthusiastic that he was thought to be mad and his disciples to be drunk and Cole thought that unless the Connexion could make room for enthusiasm it would sink within the next generation "into a mere eclectic cult without evangelistic force or national significance". He said the young would only be won by working with them in practical tasks, and he told of a group of young men, all reclaimed drunkards who gave themselves to rescuing other drunkards, especially on Saturday nights (1905, 74-9).

Another oft-mentioned factor in the growth of the young was the influence of the Christian home. Rev. John Williams put the matter quaintly in the aphorism, "A bird has many perches but one nest". He stressed the lasting effect upon children of a devout and daily reading of the Bible in the home and he said parents should insist upon their children attending family prayers even when they had no taste for it since "their natural instincts are not spiritual". Servants should also be made to feel themselves part of a Christian home. However, Williams disowned any intention of setting up a Spartan discipline because there was need of amusement and bodily exercise, especially in an age when the strain of examinations was great ; wise parents would provide their children with musical instruments and a bicycle (1897, 46-7). Rev. Richard Jones, Wiston, spoke in 1899 of the "lamentable leakage" which he attributed in part to the decay of home-training discipline. Family training in the past had often been emotional and negative rather than moral and positive but now it was becoming a thing of the past with no restraint, no influence for good, no atmosphere of reverence and generosity. Jones thought that wealth was outstripping education ; money-making and the quest for social status had driven out religion and moral earnestness, and the contemporary test was success. However, Rev. R. G. Jones, Egremont, while admitting the decay of home-training, said that this should not be made an excuse for glossing over the weaknesses in the teaching provided by the Church ; "young men worthy of the name are not to be taught the way to heaven by a kindergarten system, pleasant Sunday afternoons, sacred concerts and magic lanterns". Jones said that the Gospel ought to be presented in such a way as to stimulate thought and lead to decision ; God's great gifts were not advertised in a cheap sale but were treasures hid in a field. Jones also pled for "a manlier tone in our ministry" ; he held that the young men of the Church heartily despise "your mealy-mouthed, oily-skinned perfect people with their shallow full assurance" (1899, 47). The problem of raising the quality of teaching was difficult to solve, and even by 1925 there were complaints about its ineffectiveness. Mr. Derry Evans, M.A., said the parental responsibility had weakened and many teachers in Sunday schools wasted precious minutes discussing scandal and sport rather than the Bible (1925, 49-53).

Allied to the task of teaching in the Sunday schools was the duty of preparing the young for full membership of the Church. In 1893 Rev. Douglas Watters said that ministers should for one year forget the adults and concentrate on preaching to and visiting the young ; "our boys and girls can belong to Christ ; they do belong to him" ; Watters thought that popular preaching and more music should be found in services so as to attract the young (1893, 17). Rev. Richard Jones, Wiston, thought that ministers should give full attention to a children's class wherein the life of Christ would be taught, and he would also have a class wherein intending young Communicants would be grounded in the doctrines of the Church and in the duties of its members. He thought there was also the opportunity in such a class for instruction in the history of the Connexion, in the Confession of Faith, and in the meaning of the Church and its Sacraments. There was, in his view, need for a textbook covering this ground; it ought to avoid a narrow sectarianism or a cheap liberalism but should stress the unity and mutual responsibility of members in the Body of Christ. Sectarian isolation meant that Christians were cut off from the Body and were consequently stunted and perverted (1899, 38-40). Rev. Richard Williams, Rhos, thought that especially in the English-speaking churches there was still a good proportion of the comparatively young, and he felt that there were too few aged saints to guide the young. Like Jones he held that a knowledge of the history of the Connexion would produce a deep love for it (1899, 44). Rev. J. Calvin Thomas, Hoylake, thought that entrance to the Church was not sufficiently guarded and by making admission too easy the standard of conduct had fallen (1899, 59). Rev. J. W. Matthews, Ystrad, thought that the young were admitted to membership without sufficient instruction and without sufficient personal conviction; too many, in his view, drifted into the Church due to parental influence, due to the spell of an attractive preacher, due to social pressure, or even in hope of benefits (1899, 60). The problem was perennial and in 1930 Rev. John Edwards said there was need to stress the importance of the step to become a church member; young people ought to be made aware of the serious responsibilities involved. In Japan a candidate for membership was asked if he was prepared to die for Christ, but in Britain it was perhaps more relevant to ask whether or not a candidate was willing to live for Christ (1930, 34-7).

It was also felt by some speakers that the young members of the Church were not given a place of responsibility in the management of the Church. Rev. E. Rowland, Crickhowell, said there was no reason for reserving the office of deacon for those who "have passed the meridian of life". He also thought that the young could find useful employment in the expanding social services and in local government (1903, 45). This was not always welcomed as a means of service; Mr.

Edward Cartwright, Dowlais, said there was a risk that extraneous civic, business, philanthropic, and recreational activities could loosen the sense of obligation to the weekly Seiat (1909, 48-50).

A further light upon the outlook of the Connexion is revealed in the attitude adopted by several speakers to sport. Prof. Edwin Williams, Trevecka, said there was a mania for muscular exercises and games which threatened to become an engrossing thraldom wherein mind became subordinate to muscle (1899, 20). Rev. John Williams admitted that the pressure of study required the counteracting force of amusement and bodily exercise (1897, 46-7). Rev. R. G. Jones was more positive; "all our young men have not gone to the football field, and all who have, have not gone to the devil"; because the young are lively and gay, even what some would call frivolous, it did not follow that they were all reprobate and ungodly, and he was sure that if there was a mania for athletics there was also a thirst for God among the young (1899, 47). Rev. John Hughes, Holyhead, also admitted the value of athletics "in the right proportion" but he feared that their popularity was a sign of worldliness and was leading to the neglect of higher spiritual duties; a football match enticed the young from the weeknight service, and after Saturday's football match or cycle tour the young were allegedly too tired to attend the morning service on Sunday. He also rejected any idea that the Church should provide athletic exercise for the young, and he thought that it might indeed be the Church's duty to raise its voice against the worldly spirit spreading over the land (1899, 48-9). This opinion was much debated in future years. In 1901 Keir Hardie, M.P., said the Church was not called upon to organise amusements (1901, 50). Prof. Ellis Edwards thought much harm was done by the standoffish attitude adopted by adults towards games, and the young were given the impression that a choice had to be made between religion and sport (1899, 50). Rev. Barrow Williams spoke on the "Athletic Cult" and said it was not the Church's task to provide amusement or to draw up a list of permitted amusements, but there were certain principles which should feature in every sport permissible for the Christian. Amusement must be innocent, must give relaxation suited to various types of occupation, must not infringe on working hours, and ought not to lead into unhealthy company. Williams feared there was probably too much truth in the statement which had appeared in the *Spectator* that a second or third rate man would be preferred to a first rate man for a public-school post if he were a good football player (1901, 57-8). Rev. E. Rowland, Crickhowell, said that while there were perils in athletics the Church must not oppose amusements and recreation when taken in moderation (1903, 44).

In 1908 Mr. E. Madoc Jones, M.A., Beaumaris, said there was great need of reasonable relaxation in a strenuous age and he felt that much harm had been done by "well-meaning people in all our churches by crying down of recreations and games which are perfectly innocent in themselves" (1908, 42-3). In 1913 Mr. Ernest Evans, B.A., LL.B., Aberystwyth, was of the opinion that young people were more solemn and serious than in the past in spite of their keen interest in sport and novels (1913, 44). In 1925 Mr. Derry Evans, M.A., spoke directly about the need of taking the young seriously in the work of the Church; he thought that the children's address during a service was useless and he suggested that there should be fortnightly morning services on Sundays specially designed for children so that they might be taught the way to worship; he also said that the Church's concern for the young should not be confined to Sundays but should include weeknight clubs for intellectual, social and physical recreation, and he commended such organisations as the Boy Scouts and the Boys' Brigade (1925, 51-3). In 1934 Rev. Howell Williams, Cardiff, said that the present age was obsessed with athleticism (1934, 29).

It cannot be deduced from these references that speakers were enthusiastic devotees of sport. While they knew in their mind that there was nothing inherently evil in sport yet deep down in their being they had suspicions of sport and believed it could be a diversion from more important things. The passing years have seen the growth of a more positive attitude to the value of sport but it cannot be said that their fears were without foundation.

In all its discussions the Conferences were aware that Welsh Presbyterianism was facing an uncertain future and that the young people, who would eventually become members and leaders of the Church, would have to assume their responsibilities in a very uncertain future. The ferment in the world of thought was forcing a reappraisal of dogma. The former zest for denominational strife seemed to be ebbing into a paralysis which recognised that denominationalism was difficult to reconcile with the New Testament pattern of the Church, but which was equally impotent to enter upon any new or living way. Moreover, with the widening of human horizons and the opening of a vast new range of occupations, local churches were losing much of their prestige as social and educational centres. Also, the turbulent condition of world affairs and the rise of the European dictators provided an overcast prospect. In these circumstances it was difficult to provide sure guidance for the young, and not many speeches can be regarded as a sparkling or forward-looking challenge to the young. Indeed, few, if any, of the difficulties facing the denomination in the period of the Conferences have been triumphantly solved.

APPENDIX I

CONFERENCES OF ENGLISH CHURCHES IN THE PRESBYTERIAN CHURCH OF WALES

No.	Year	Place	President	Preacher or Visiting Speaker
1.	1899	Bath St., Aberystwyth	Rev. Principal T. C. Edwards	Rev. John McNeill, Regent Sq., London
2.	1892	Catharine St., Liverpool	Rev. Wm. Powell, Pembroke	Rev. John Robertson, Glasgow
3.	1893	Havelock St., Newport	Dr. Ebenezer Davies, M.O.H., Swansea	Rev. James Stalker, D.D., Glasgow
4.	1894	City Road, Chester	Rev. Dr. J. Cynddylan Jones, Cardiff	Rev. Prof. G. Adam Smith, Glasgow
5.	1895	Cardiff	Mr. E. J. Baillie, F.L.S., Chester	Rev. F. B. Meyer, London
6.	1896	Oswestry	Rev. Wm. Evans, M.A., Pembroke Dock	Rev. Dr. J. Guiness Rogers, London
7.	1897	Argyle, Swansea	Mr. William Evans, J.P., Southport	Rev. Prof. James Denney, Glasgow
8.	1898	Oakfield Road, Liverpool	Rev. Edwin Williams, M.A., Vice-Principal Trevecka College	Rev. Dr. G. C. Lorimer, Tremont Temple, Boston
9.	1899	Abergavenny	Rev. Ellis Edwards, M.A., Vice-Principal Bala	Rev. Alexander Connell, London
10.	1900	Llandudno	Ald. J. Jones Griffiths, Penygraig	Rev. William Watson, Birkenhead
11.	1901	Merthyr Tydfil	Mr. J. R. Davies, M.A., J.P., Menai Bridge	Rev. Prin. P. T. Forsyth, London
12.	1902	Hill Street, Wrexham	Rev. Prin. Owen Prys, M.A., Trevecka	Rev. Hugh Black, Edinburgh
13.	1903	Llanelli	Rev. D. Lloyd Jones, M.A., Llandinam	
14.	1904	Ala Road, Pwllheli	Mr. Augustus Lewis, Manchester	Rev. James Travis, Chester
15.	1905	Penarth	Rev. Joseph Evans, Denbigh	Rev. Dr. James Stalker, Aberdeen (2nd visit)
16.	1906	Shrewsbury	Mr. Evan Davies, Port Talbot	Rev. J. H. Jowett, M.A., Birmingham

No.	Year	Place	President	Preacher or Visiting Speaker
17.	1907	Pontypridd	Rev. Edward Parry, M.A., Newtown	Rev. W. L. Watkinson, London
18.	1908	Colwyn Bay	Rev. J. Glyn Davies, Rhyl	Rev. Dr. G. Campbell Morgan, London
19.	1909	Llandrindod Wells	Sir J. Herbert Roberts, Bt., M.P.	Rev. Dr. David Smith, Blairgowrie
20.	1910	Liscard	Alderman S. N. Jones, J.P., Newport	Rev. W. M. Clow, Glasgow
21.	1911	Bethany, Port Talbot	Rev. T. G. Owen, M.A., Liverpool	Rev. J. D. Jones, Bournemouth
22.	1912	Machynlleth	Rev. R. R. Roberts, B.A., Chester	Rev. T. Phillips, B.A., Bloomsbury
23.	1913	Aberdare	Mr. John Owens, J.P., Chester (in place of Rev. W. M. Jenkins who died before the Conference)	Rev. Dr. R. F. Horton, London
24.	1919	City Road, Chester	Rev. Wm. Mendus, Cardiff	Rev. Dr. J. A. Hutton, Glasgow
25.	1920	Corporation Rd., Newport	Rev. R. G. Jones, Liverpool	Rev. James Reid, Eastbourne
26.	1921	Prince's Road, Bangor	Rev. J. Ceredig Evans, India	Rev. Dr. W. E. Orchard, London
27.	1922	Rhyddings Pk., Swansea	Sir Henry Lewis (absent due to illness)	Rev. Dr. H. Maldwyn Hughes, Cambridge
28.	1923	Hoylake	Rev. T. C. Jones, Penarth	Very Rev. Prof. W. M. McGregor, Glasgow
29.	1924	Cathedral Rd., Cardiff	Rev. A. Wynne Thomas, Wrexham	Rev. Prin. W. B. Selbie, Oxford
30.	1925	Llandudno	Rev. E. P. Jones, B.A., Cardiff	Rev. T. Rhondda Williams, Brighton
31.	1926	Llanelli	Rev. T. W. Reese, India	Rev. Prof. James Moffat, Glasgow
32.	1927	Newtown	Rev. D. M. Rees, Tredegar	Rev. Dr. S. W. Hughes, London
33.	1928	Pontypridd	Rev. J. H. Davies, Ewloe Green	Rev. Dr. R. C. Gillie, Bath
34.	1929	Princes Street, Rhyl	Rev. J. Morgan Jones, M.A., Merthyr	Rev. Arthur Hird, London
35.	1930	Merthyr Tydfil	Rev. John Edwards, Wrexham	Very Rev. Dr. Harry Miller, Edinburgh

No.	Year	Place	President	Preacher or Visiting Speaker
36.	1931	Wrexham	Rev. R. J. Rees, M.A., Cardiff	Rev. F. C. Spurr, Birmingham
37.	1932	London Road, Neath	Rev. John Roberts, Wrexham	Rev. Ex-Principal E. Griffith Jones, Bradford
38.	1933	Catharine St., Liverpool	Mr. T. G. Dew, Cardiff	
39.	1934	Bath Street, Aberystwyth	Rev. R. R. Williams, M.A., Chester	Rev. G. T. Bellhouse, London
40.	1935	Colwyn Bay	Rev. F. W. Cole, Cardiff	Rev. Prof. D. S. Cairns, Aberdeen
41.	1936	Cardiff Memorial Hall	Rev. Dr. Richard Llandinam (Jones)	Rev. Gwilym O. Griffith, Birmingham
42.	1937	Bethel Street, Llanidloes	Dr. H. Gordon Roberts India	Rev. Prof. H. H. Farmer, Cambridge
43.	1938	Argyle, Swansea	Rev. R. J. Rees, M.A., Cardiff	Rev. J. Ernest James, London

APPENDIX II

BIBLIOGRAPHY

Series of Conference Reports, 1889—1938
The Monthly Treasury.
Y Goleuad (The Denominational Weekly).
Y Blwyddiadur (The Denominational Yearbook).
Gweithrediadau y Gymanfa Gyffredinol (Minutes of the General Assembly).
Y Bywgraffiadur Cymraeg. (Also English Edition)
Deg o Enwogion (dwy gyfres).

APPENDIX III

NOTES

Chapter I

1. Nuttall, G., *Howel Harris, the last Enthusiast* ; Knox, R. B., "Howell Harris and his Doctrine of the Church" (CCH, 1964-5).
2. Edwards, T. C., *Bywyd a Llythyrau Lewis Edwards* ; Evans, Trebor Lloyd, *Lewis Edwards : Ei fywyd a'i waith* ; Knox, R. B., "Lewis Edwards", in *The London Quarterly and Holborn Review*, Jan. 1964.
3. See Appendix III.
4. *Y Goleuad*, Medi (Sept.) 27, 1899, p. 8 ; Hydref (Oct.) 24, 1900, p. 8 ; Medi 25, 1907, p. 12.
5. Ibid, Hydref 3, 1902, p. 9.
6. Ibid., Hydref 6, 1892, p. 8.
7. Ibid, Medi 22, 1893.
8. Ibid., Hydref 2, 1901, p. 9.
9. Davies, E. T., *Religion in the Industrial Revolution in South Wales*, p. 152.
10. Articles in BC, in *The Monthly Treasury* (May, 1900) and in Nicoll, W. R., *Princes of the Church*.
11. Articles in BC.
12. *Y Goleuad*, Medi 18, 1895, p. 8.
13. Article in BC.
14. Article in BC.
15. Davies, E. T., op. cit., pp. 40 and 45.
16. *Gweithrediadau Y Gymanfa Gyffredinol*, 1891, p. 44; *Y Blwyddiadur* 1920, p. 94.
17. *Y Blwyddiadur*, 1936.

Chapter II

1. Article in BC.
2. *Y Goleuad*, Medi 19, 1894, p. 2.

Chapter III

1. Article in BC ; see Hanson, R.P.C., *Saint Patrick*.
2. *Y Goleuad*, Hydref 2, 1907, p. 12.
3. Article in BC.
4. Article in *Deg o Enwogion* (Ail gyfres).
5. Ibid.
6. Article in BC.
7. Official history by J. C. Pollock.
8. Article in BC.

Chapter V

1. Article in BC.
2. *Y Goleuad*, Hydref 2, 1901, p. 9.
3. Article in BC.

Chapter VI

1. Davies, G. M.Ll., *Pilgrimage of Peace* with Memoir by C. E. Raven. Griffith, E. H., *Heddychwr Mawr Cymru* (Cyf. I).

INDEX OF CONFERENCE SPEAKERS

Armstrong, Rev. E., 47, 57, 67.
Astley, Rev. C. T., 62.

Baillie, E. J., 61, 123.
Baillie, Rev. J., 75.
Belden, Rev. A. D., 87.
Brace, W., 109.
Brooke-Gwynne, Canon C., 78.
Brown, Ald. C., 76.

Cartwright, E., 38, 132.
Clothier, Rev. W. J., 65
Clow, Rev. W. M., 85.
Cole, Rev. F. W., 52, 117, 129.
Cromar, G., 92.

Davies, Rev. Prin. D. C., 40, 61.
Davies, Dr. E., 29, 71, 79, 91.
Davies, E., 90.
Davies, Rev. E. O., 64.
Davies, Rev. I. O., 54.
Davies, Rev. G. M. Ll., 114, 118, 125.
Davies, Rev. J. G., 14, 19, 23, 31, 38, 67, 77, 91, 98, 109.
Davies, Rev. J. H., 53, 76, 116, 128.
Davies, Rev. J. R., 99.
Davies, J. R., 68, 75, 102.
Davies, Rev. J. T., 102, 110.
Davies, R., 116.
Davies, Rev. T., 58.
Davies, T., 101.
Davies, T. A., 29.
Davies, Sir Walford, 31.
Davies, Rev. Prof., W. D., 55.
Davies, Rev. W., 74.
Davies, Rev. W. W., 98.
Denney, Rev. Prof. J., 83.
Dew, T. G., 25.

Edwards, Rev. D. C., 17, 54, 68, 71, 76, 81.
Edwards, Rev. Prof. E., 15, 38, 49, 51, 61, 66, 89, 97, 105, 132.

Edwards, Rev. Prof. G. A., 52, 65,
Edwards, Rev. J., 37, 76, 82, 107, 116 124, 131.
Edwards, Rev. Prin. T. C., 15, 17 18, 19, 43, 49, 60, 83.
Ellis, Rev. G., 104.
Evans, D., 124, 130, 133.
Evans, Rev. D. T., 127.
Evans, Rev. E., 95, 102.
Evans, Ernest, 101, 133.
Evans, Evan, 101.
Evans, Rev. G. H., 37.
Evans, Rev. J., 14, 92.
Evans, Rev. J. D., 16, 17, 109.
Evans, Rev. Prof. J. Y., 42, 81.
Evans, R. D., 29.
Evans, Miss T., 127.
Evans, Rev. W., 13.
Evans, W., 73, 82, 123.
Evans, W. R., 57.

Farmer, Rev. Dr. H. H., 88.
Fleming, Rev. Dr. J. R., 86.
Forsyth, Rev. Dr. P. T., 84.

Gillie, Rev. Dr. R. C., 87.
Glynne, Rev. W., 126.
Gray, Rev. T., 42.
Green, Rev. T. M., 90.
Griffiths, Ald. J. J., 42, 72, 97, 126.
Griffiths, Rev. M., 123, 128.

Hardie, K., 100, 132.
Harding, Prof. E. W., 27.
Harris, D., 39.
Harris, J. M., 16, 32, 78, 82, 111.
Henderson, A., 102.
Howard, Rev. J. H., 47, 103, 113.
Howe, D., 118.
Hughes, Rev. Prin. H. H., 53.
Hughes, Dr. H. L., 82.
Hughes, Rev. J., 56, 81, 94, 122, 126, 132.

INDEX

Hughes, Prin. J., 125.
Hughes, Rev. J. E., 40.
Hughes, Rev. J. R., 19, 73.
Hughes, Rev. R., 64, 72, 109.
Hutton, Rev. Dr. J. A., 85.

James, Rev. D., 53.
James, Rev. E., 46.
James, Rev. W. (Manchester), 72.
James, Rev. W. (Aberdare), 40, 42.
Jenkins, Rev. A. J., 91.
Jenkins, Rev. J. L., 17, 56, 58.
Jones, Rev. A., 70.
Jones, Rev. D. E. Ll., 78.
Jones, Rev. D. Ll., 57, 61.
Jones, E., 80.
Jones, E. M., 124, 133.
Jones, E. W., 127.
Jones, Rev. Dr. J. Cynddylan, 15, 19, 31, 33, 41, 44, 55, 76, 79, 93.
Jones, Rev. Dr. J. M., 35, 93.
Jones, Rev. J. M., 17, 44, 64, 94, 106, 115.
Jones, Rev. J. P., 47, 77, 102, 123.
Jones, Rev. J. V., 89, 92.
Jones, Rev. P. J., 70.
Jones, Rev. Dr. R., 55, 111, 118, 120, 126, 128.
Jones, Rev. R. G., 60, 96, 100, 102, 130, 132.
Jones, S. G., 103.
Jones, Ald. S. N., 23, 77, 96, 97, 128.
Jones, Rev. T., 98.
Jones, Rev. T. C., 59, 106.
Jones, W., 22.
Jones, Prof. W. J., 126.
Jones, Rev. W. S., 41.
Joshua, Rev. S., 35, 90.

Levi, Prof. T. A., 37, 94, 117.
Lewis, A., 23, 29, 30, 93, 109.
Lewis, Rev. C. J., 92.
Lewis, E. P., 100.
Lewis, H., 124.
Lewis, Sir J. H., 99, 107, 110.
Lewis, Rev. W., 127.

Lewis, Rev. W. W., 48
Lloyd, D., 22.
Lloyd, Mrs. W., 126.
Lloyd-Jones, Rev. Dr. D. M., 56.
Lorimer, Rev. Dr. G. C., 84.
Lundie, Rev. Dr. R. H., 97.

MacNeill, Rev. J., 83.
Matthews, B., 87.
Matthews, Rev. J. W., 131.
Mendus, Rev. E. L., 117.
Mendus, Rev. W., 112.
Mercer, Rt. Rev. Bp., 77.
Meyler, H. H., 92, 127.
Miles, Rev. E. G., 82, 110.
Morgan, J., 28.
Morgan, Rev. J. J., 81.
Morgan, Rev. R. H., 18, 90.
Morgan, Rev. S. O., 38.
Morris, Dr. O.,
Morris, Rev. R., 13, 48.

Orchard, Rev. Dr. W. E., 86.
Owen, Rev. D. S., 117.
Owen, Rev. Jas., 13, 79.
Owen, Rev. John, 126.
Owen, Rev. J. H., 68, 95.
Owen, O., 13, 71, 105.
Owen, Rev. T. G., 23, 62, 80, 98, 99, 110.
Owens, J., 14, 24, 38, 67, 69, 82, 99, 110, 124.

Parry, Rev. E., 16, 19, 20, 35.
Phillips, Rev. Prof. D., 44, 46, 54, 60,
Phillips, Rev. I., 66.
Powell, Rev. R. L., 16.
Prys, Rev. Prin. O., 13, 15, 19, 48, 63, 67, 69, 77, 80, 89.
Pugh, Rev. Dr. J., 89, 90, 98.
Pugh, Mrs. J., 123.

Rees, Rev. D., 79.
Rees, Rev. D. M., 32, 36, 65, 114.
Rees, E., 39.
Rees, Rev. H., 75.

INDEX

Rees, Rev. R. J., 44, 80, 124, 128.
Rees, Rev. T., 34, 71.
Reynolds, G. P., 90.
Roberts, Rev. B., 46.
Roberts, Very Rev. G., 78.
Roberts, Rev. J. (Cardiff), 20, 117.
Roberts, Rev. J. (Chester), 18.
Roberts, J. H. (Lord Clwyd), 97, 109.
Roberts, Rev. R. M., 69.
Roberts, Rev. R. R., 35, 64, 67, 80, 82, 90, 105, 106.
Rogers, Rev. Dr. J. G., 83.
Rowland, Rev. E., 30, 123, 131, 133.

Saunders, Rev. J. M., 44, 58, 72, 75, 93.
Saunders, Mrs. J. M., 107.
Smith, Rev. Dr. D., 85.
Smith, Rev. Prof. G. A., 83.

Thomas, Rev. A. W., 52, 58, 73, 74, 95, 96, 98, 109.
Thomas, Rev. D. O. C., 21, 116.
Thomas, Rev. G., 17, 59.
Thomas, Rev. J. C., 13, 21, 38, 55, 131.
Thomas, Rev. J. J., 42.
Thomas, Rev. Prof. J. O., 50.
Thomas, M., 108.
Thomas, T. C., 127.
Travis, Rev. J., 73, 76, 82.
Turner, H., 127.

Vaughan, Mrs. G., 97, 99.

Watson, Rev. J., 108.
Watters, Rev. J. D., 122, 123, 130.
Wheldon, Rev. T. J., 72.
Wheldon, Major W. P., 112.
Williams, Rev. C. V., 50, 65, 69.
Williams, Rev. Prof. D., 51, 52.
Williams, Rev. D. D., 76.
Williams, Rev. Prof. E., 13, 32, 61, 132.
Williams, Rev. E., 55, 72.
Williams, Very Rev. G., 88.
Williams, Rev. G. P., 16.
Williams, Rev. Howell (Cardiff), 116, 133.
Williams, Rev. Howell (Hoylake), 117.
Williams, Rev. Prof. H., 43.
Williams, Rev. H. B., 38, 108, 132.
Williams, Rev. J. (Chester), 27.
Williams, Rev. J. (Dolgellau), 91.
Williams, Rev. M. W., 59, 104, 114, 119.
Williams, Rev. R. J., 13.
Williams, Rev. R. R., 15, 26.
Williams, Rev. W., 62, 66.
Williams, W. H., 115.
Williams, Rev. W. W., 49.
Wilson, Prebendary, 78.

Yates, Rev. T., 113.